Open Heart

With Open Heart

Spiritual Direction in the Alphonsian Tradition

DENNIS J. BILLY, C.SS.R.

Liguori
LIGUORI, MISSOURI

Published by Liguori Publications
Liguori, Missouri
www.liguori.org
www.catholicbooksonline.com

Imprimi Potest:
Richard Thibodeau, C.Ss.R.
Provincial, Denver Province
The Redemptorists

Library of Congress Cataloging-in-Publication Data

Billy, Dennis Joseph.
    With open heart : spiritual direction in the Alphonsian tradition /
Dennis J. Billy.
        p. cm.
    Includes bibliographical references.
    ISBN 0-7648-1090-1 (pbk.)
    1. Spirtual direction. 2. Liguori, Alfonso Maria de', Saint, 1696–
1787. I. Title.

BX2350.7.B44 2003
253.5'3—dc21   2003044621

Printed in the United States of America
07 06 05 04 03   5 4 3 2

For Carl Hoegerl, C.Ss.R.
and
Walter Karrer, C.Ss.R.
—in appreciation

⌒∞⌒

Treat with him of your business, your plans, your griefs, your fears—of all that concerns you. Above all, do so (as I have said) with confidence, with open heart.

ALPHONSUS DE LIGUORI

Saint Alphonsus was highly distinguished by his charism for spiritual direction, and our tradition has always held it in high esteem. It is exceptionally important in our times when people are given to such continual self-questioning. This ministry must be given new forms suitable to the mentality of the people of today....

REDEMPTORIST C&S
GENERAL STATUTE 024

CONTENTS

Acknowledgments

Parts of this book were previously published as: "An Alphonsian Model of Spiritual Direction," in *Proceedings of the Fifth International Congress of Redemptorist Moral Theologians Held in Materdomini, Italy 7–12 July 2002,* ed. Raymond Douziech (Rome, 2002): 123–49; "A Redemptorist Model of Spiritual Direction," *Spiritus Patris* 28 (no. 1, 2002): 11–14; "Fostering a Communion of Traditions and the Ministry of Spiritual Direction," *Pastoral Life* 51 (no. 3, 2002): 12-18; "Saint Alphonsus and Today's Spiritual Direction," *Review for Religious* 61 (2002): 242–51; "St. Alphonsus de Liguori: Doctor of Prayer," *The Priest* 58 (no. 8, 2002): 42–44.

INTRODUCTION

Does the spiritual doctrine of Alphonsus de Liguori (1696–1787), founder of the Redemptorists, doctor of prayer, and patron saint of confessors and moral theologians, have anything to offer today's spiritual directors as they seek deeper insights into the nature of their ministry? Can his teachings offer directors anything that will enable them to practice their craft with more competence and heightened pastoral concern? Can they provide directors with insights into how they can help others to listen and respond to the gentle movements of the Spirit deep within their hearts? Answering such questions is more difficult than many of us might first be willing to admit. The spiritual landscape of eighteenth-century Naples and its environs was very different from our own. Some of the most basic presuppositions of Alphonsus's approach to spiritual direction (for example, its highly directive nature, its close link with sacramental reconciliation) are questioned by many involved in the ministry today, if not outrightly opposed.

What is more, today's spiritual directors are likely to be men and women from all walks of life, a stark contrast to the predominantly clerical influence upon the ministry that was prominent in Alphonsus's day. In many circles, moreover, the phrase "spiritual direction" has itself given way to more nondirective expressions, such as "spiritual guidance" and "spiritual accompaniment." Such changes give witness to the radical shift in the approach taken towards spiritual direction over the last twenty-five to thirty years. Today, the ministry is much more interdisciplinary and ecumenical than it was in the eighteenth century, so much so that one may wonder if Alphonsus has anything at all to offer spiritual directors whose approach to their ministry is so very different from his own.

My purpose in this book is to find appropriate points of contact between Alphonsus's spiritual legacy and the ministry of spiritual direction as it is understood and practiced today by a growing number of dedicated Christians. Doing so will require a particular interpretive stance toward the Alphonsian tradition, one that can best be understood by taking a close look at the three meanings of the Greek word for "interpretation" (that is, *hermēneuein*): (1) to say, (2) to explain, and (3) to translate.[1]

The first connotation of this word can be rendered "expressing aloud in words,"and, by way of analogy, "the determination of what was said." When applied to the Alphonsian tradition, it refers to that important work of historians who seek to discover the relevant texts of Alphonsus's writings and make them available to the public in carefully researched critical editions. While much progress has been made in this area of Alphonsian studies, a great deal still needs to be accomplished. To be sure, Alphonsus wrote so much and on such a variety of topics that a complete critical edition of all of his Latin and Italian works still waits to see the light of day.[2]

The second connotation of *hermēneuein* has to do with explaining a particular situation, or interpreting the meaning of a text. When applied to the Alphonsian tradition, it refers to those attempts by scholars to identify the circumstances of Alphonsus's life so that his various writings can be interpreted in an appropriate historical context. A thorough knowledge of the historical backdrop against which Alphonsus lived and worked can have a tremendous impact on understanding his writings. The modern biographers of Alphonsus have done a great service to us by providing such thorough human portraits of this great missionary figure.[3]

Still another connotation of *hermēneuein* has to do with translating. When applied to the Alphonsian tradition, this final meaning takes on two dimensions. In the first place, it refers to the efforts of scholars to provide accurate and readable translations of Alphonsus's works in other languages. Some of Alphonsus's works have had the good fortune of being translated into a number of foreign languages; others, however, have never been translated, and perhaps never will. Today's English readers can benefit greatly from the nineteenth-century edition of Alphonsus's ascetical works edited by Eugene Grimm and by recent anthologies of his writings such as Carl Hoegerl's *Heart Calls to Heart* and the one edited by Frederick Jones for the *Classics of Western Spirituality* series. Liguori Publications, moreover, has done us a service by putting out new editions and popular translations of *The Practice of the Love of Jesus Christ* and *The Glories of Mary*.[4]

In the second place, this connotation of the word also has to do with translating Alphonsus's spiritual legacy so that it can be passed on in a meaningful way from one generation to the next. This work of translation is every bit as difficult as putting Alphonsus's words into a foreign language, perhaps more. It involves finding appropriate elements in Alphonsus's teaching that can be extracted and then analogously applied to the needs of today's believing community. Doing so requires an ongoing dialogue between past and present. It also means bringing a flexible yet highly focused interpretive eye to the situation so that the insights of Alphonsus can be creatively applied to circumstances very different from his own.

In this book, I will follow this last understanding of the Greek word *hermēneuein*. As such, I will seek to develop and draw out useful parallels between Alphonsus's spiritual teachings and the present-day ministry of spiritual direction. For reasons already hinted at, however, I will look not to Alphonsus's teaching on spiritual direction itself, but to his teaching on prayer, specifically to his particular approach to the manner of making mental prayer. I do so not to denigrate Alphonsus's own teaching on direction (it still has much to offer us), but to move that tradition forward so that it can speak to the spiritual needs of today's believing community in more practical and relevant ways. I will do so by arguing that the dynamics involved in Alphonsus's simple and practical way of conversing familiarly with God can be extended to the direction process itself and form the basis of an updated Alphonsian approach to the ministry of spiritual direction.

Helpful points of historical correlation can arise in the most surprising and unexpected of places. To find these helpful connections, however, today's translators of Alphonsus's spiritual legacy need to have one foot firmly planted in his world as well as their own. The book's six chapters seek to do just that. Each stands alone but also builds on the insights of whatever may precede it. When taken as a whole, they offer a creative pastoral introduction to a model of spiritual direction that, at one and the same time, is both faithful to the Alphonsian tradition and able to speak to the hearts and minds of those seeking direction today. The content of these chapters verifies this claim.

In chapter one, "Spiritual Direction, Toward a Communion of Traditions," I provide a broad panoramic view of the various traditions of spiritual direction in the Christian tradition and argue for the importance of naming one's tradition and taking ownership of it. Doing so often means adapting it in such a way so that circumstances unforeseen by earlier generations can be incorporated into the tradition and dealt with appropriately.

In chapter two, "Saint Alphonsus: Spiritual Master," I look at the basis for Alphonsus's reputation as a spiritual master by studying the vast array of influences that helped him to produce a Gospel spirituality that was simple, apostolic, and creatively eclectic in its approach to the spiritual life. Special emphasis is given to his understanding of the confessor-director's role in leading people to sanctity.

In chapter three, "Saint Alphonsus and Prayer," I examine the saint's teaching on prayer. I do so by pointing out his understanding the various grades of prayer as it filtered down to him (most notably through the Carmelite tradition) and then by focusing on his strong pastoral emphasis on prayer as the great means of salvation. Within this context, I look at Alphonsus's insistence on the moral necessity of mental prayer for fostering in one's life an intimate relationship with God.

In chapter four, "Saint Alphonsus and the Manner of Making Mental Prayer," I study Alphonsus's approach to mental prayer in more detail. In it, I deal not only with Alphonsus's unique contribution to the Christian tradition on this type of prayer, but also go into the various theological reasons for understanding its importance for our lives.

In chapter five, "An Alphonsian Model of Spiritual Direction," I apply the dynamics of Alphonsus's approach to mental prayer to the process of spiritual direction itself. In it, I argue that the manner of making mental prayer promoted by Alphonsus has great relevance for the way his followers today should understand and implement their approach to the ministry of spiritual direction today.

Finally, in chapter six, "Some Practical Concerns," I deal with questions surrounding the effectiveness of this new model of direction and what its implementation might mean for the ministry of those wishing to pursue it. In addition to making appropriate observations on each step of the process, I also treat such issues as expectations, training, needed skills, and supervision.

To facilitate further reflection on this new proposal I have also included a series of reflection questions at the end of each chapter. The purpose of these questions is to help the readers judge what relevance this adaptation of Alphonsus's spiritual doctrine to current practices in spiritual direction might have for his or her own practice of the ministry. They are meant to serve as a practical resource for anyone interested in delving more deeply into this interesting exercise of historical translation. Two prayers of Alphonsus to the Holy Spirit are also included: one for wisdom at the beginning of the book and a humble supplication at the end. These remind us not only of Alphonsus's great devotion to the Holy Spirit but also of the important role the Spirit plays in our sanctification and in the entire direction process.

To my mind, the Alphonsian tradition has much to offer today's spiritual directors as they seek to help others to become themselves in their faith. The model presented in these pages understands that the dynamics of prayer fostered in a person's relationship with God can be transposed onto the process of direction itself and used to give that person deeper insights into the inner workings of his or her own spiritual life. When seen in this light, this new approach to spiritual direction is nothing but an extrapolation onto the plane of spiritual direction of some of Alphonsus's finest insights regarding the nature of prayer.

If this important connection between Alphonsus's approach to mental prayer and spiritual direction has not been discovered until now, it may be because the students of Alphonsus's spiritual legacy were concentrating on other relevant (and highly necessary) tasks associated with the art of interpretation (that is, *hermēneuein*). If this is so, one can only conclude that the time is now ripe to translate the Alphonsian tradition in such a way so that it can speak insightfully and with power to the people seeking direction in their lives today. My purpose in this book—to draw an appropriate historical correlation between Alphonsus's approach to mental prayer and our current understanding of the practice of spiritual direction—is but one example of the kind of historical connections we should be looking for.

PRAYER TO THE HOLY SPIRIT (I)

Holy Spirit, Divine Consoler! I adore you as my true God, just as I adore God the Father and God the Son. I bless you by uniting myself to the blessings that you receive from the angels and the seraphs. I offer you my whole heart, and I give you heartfelt thanks for all the benefits that you have bestowed and continue to bestow upon the world. You who are the author of all supernatural gifts and who enriched with immense favors the soul of the Blessed Virgin Mary the Mother of God, I beseech you to visit me with your grace and your love and to grant me the gift of Wisdom, so that I may be able to direct all my actions by referring them to God as my last end. By loving and serving you in this life as I ought, may I have the happiness of eternally possessing you in the next.

ALPHONSUS DE LIGUORI

Chapter One

SPIRITUAL DIRECTION, TOWARD A COMMUNION OF TRADITIONS

When understood under the general heading of the "care for and cure of souls," spiritual direction encompasses virtually every aspect of the Church's pastoral ministry. Preaching, teaching, celebrating the sacraments, visiting the sick—*any* activity whose ultimate goal is to help people draw closer to Christ can be thought of as a type of spiritual guidance or accompaniment.

When taken in the more specific sense, however, of "a helping relationship focusing on a person's growth in the spiritual life," it displays unique characteristics in its own right and emerges as a highly specialized ministry.[1] Gaining a sense of the historical development of this second, more traditional understanding of the ministry is no easy task. In a short presentation of this kind, we can only hope to point out some of the common pitfalls to be avoided and some broad considerations relevant to our specific interests.

SOME DIFFICULTIES

When examining the history of Christian spiritual direction, we need to avoid giving the impression that it developed in a strictly linear fashion, as if out of necessity, through a number of succinct (albeit clearly related and successive) stages. To do so would be to subject the movement and growth of its various theories and practices to a preconceived pattern and leave little room for human creativity. As one author puts it, we should not assume that spiritual direction is "...a monolithic tradition extending from the desert fathers to the present day, a set of practices with only minor variations over the centuries."[2] Rather, it involves a great number of diversely related spiritual traditions.

Some of these traditions have been in contact for centuries in a variety of rich and mutually beneficial ways. Others have only recently begun to reap the benefits of critical dialogue with other approaches. Still others have had only limited outside contact and are cautious of even slight innovations. Given these varying levels of interaction, it would make more sense for us to focus on the great many forms that spiritual direction has taken down through the centuries rather than attempting to devise an artificial construction of dubious historical value.

The challenge is to be sensitive to the interrelated nature of historical events, while at the same time discerning enough to recognize original insights that make a genuine contribution to the ministry. Walking this fine line is rarely easy. It requires a keen historical sense and the use of a metaphor that emphasizes the enriching role of diversity in the ongoing development of this important ministry.

STREAMS OF INFLUENCE

In light of the above reflection, a broad panoramic view of the movement of spiritual direction within Christianity might give us a sense of the various factors involved in its development. According to Tilden Edwards, the history of Christian spiritual direction flows as a single river branching off into three streams: the Roman Catholic, the Protestant, and the Orthodox. Each of these streams carries certain *gems* in its waters that, when retrieved, can be very helpful to all involved:

> The Roman Catholic branch of spiritual direction …needs the Protestant *gems* of preaching, Bible study, pastoral counseling, and small group prayer. The Protestant branch of spiritual direction needs the Catholic *gems* of liturgy, confession, retreats, and the Christian calendar. Both the Catholic and Protestant branches need the *gem* of mystical depth which is contained in the Orthodox branch.[3]

Although these remarks embrace the broader understanding of spiritual direction as any practice that furthers the "care for and cure of souls," they also provide us with some keen insights into the contribution each of these traditions have made to the more specific understanding of the ministry.

Within the Catholic tradition, for example, spiritual direction was for centuries strongly directive and closely tied to the role of confessor. Even though the two ministries were not strictly identified, it was encouraged that one's confessor and spiritual director be the same person—and therefore a priest. Although exceptions to this rule surely existed, progress in the spiritual life generally presupposed first confronting one's inner darkness and receiving healing through sacramental reconciliation. This process of purgation was a prerequisite for the later stages of the spiritual journey and was an integral part of a person's ongoing conversion.[4]

The Orthodox tradition, in turn, recognized the importance of sacramental reconciliation, but also highlighted the role of the *starets* or spiritual father. This experienced spiritual guide was often a monk with a reputation for sanctity and who, knowing the ways of the heart, could introduce his disciples to the practice of unceasing prayer (cf. 1 Thess 5:17). More often than not, it was the *hesychast* method of prayer that became the central focus of his teachings. This method emphasizes the repetitive use of the Jesus Prayer (Lord Jesus, have mercy on me) as a way of offering one's body, soul, and spirit to God.[5]

More recently, the Protestant tradition developed and gave legitimacy to the role of the pastoral counselor in the Church. Often nonordained laymen or laywomen, the counselors used therapeutic techniques as a way of helping a person focus on and deal with concrete problems in his or her life. While the pastoral counselor was not a spiritual director in the strict sense of the word, his or her use of modern psychology in a recognized Church ministry paved the way for its eventual integration into spiritual direction and other helping relationships.[6]

This simple description of these important influences on spiritual direction provides us with some valuable insights into the current understanding of the ministry. Today's directors are men and women, ordained and nonordained, from all walks of life. They are generally an eclectic bunch who have little difficulty complementing their understanding of their ministry with insights from each of these important streams of Christian wisdom. They recognize, for example, the close historical ties between spiritual direction and sacramental reconciliation, but also see how the two ministries can benefit from clearly defined boundaries. They understand that spiritual direction is about helping a person to become oneself in his or her faith and thus see the importance of being knowledgeable in theology, experienced in the ways of the heart, and practiced in prayer. They also feel free to incorporate the insights of psychology into their ministry, but do so only to the extent that it will shed light on the nature of a person's relationship with

God. Their tendency to embrace a nondirective style in the ministry and their reliance on some kind of supervision also demonstrate the influence of the therapeutic model in their work.[7]

This mingling of traditions has greatly enriched both directors and the people they serve. Encouraged to be a genuine help to those they serve, directors have combed other traditions and borrowed whatever they think can be put to concrete, practical use. Such benefits, however, often come with their own set of risks and special challenges.

NAMING ONE'S TRADITION

Before reaping the benefits of another tradition, directors should first be clear about the essential elements of their own. Otherwise, they may find themselves adrift in a vast sea of ideas and practices with few stars to guide them and no rudder to steer them safely toward shore. To avoid such a situation, they should avert to and seriously reflect upon the particular theological tradition that has shaped their outlook toward spiritual accompaniment. Doing so will enable them to be themselves before those they are seeking to help. It will also give them the necessary criteria for discerning what elements within their tradition are nonnegotiable.

It is important for directors to name and take ownership of the particular tradition to which they belong. While they should be open enough to incorporate valid insights from other traditions (and thus enabling their own to develop), they should not be so malleable as to allow every passing fad and flashy new technique to influence their understanding and approach to their ministry. Doing so could water down their understanding of and adherence to their own tradition and, if care is not taken, leave them with little or no substance in which to anchor themselves.

As far as the Catholic tradition is concerned, it is important for directors to remember that diverse traditions of spiritual direction were (and still are) preserved in very structured and specific ways. One author puts it this way, "...for centuries the western Church managed to maintain a plurality of theological approaches to spirituality and direction by taking them as they arose and sequestering them in distinct and separate religious orders."[8] Orders such as the Benedictines, Carthusians, Franciscans, Dominicans, Carmelites, Jesuits, and Redemptorists, to name but a few, all have something to offer the ministry of spiritual direction. The Benedictines, for example, give us *lectio divina* and remind us of the centrality of the liturgy to the spiritual life. The Carthusians emphasize silence and the way of unknowing. The Franciscans offer the witness of holy simplicity. The Dominicans, in turn, provide us with their rich teaching on the theological and cardinal virtues. The Carmelites give us their teaching on mysticism and the dark night of the soul. The Jesuits present us with their spiritual exercises, helping us to appreciate the role of the imagination for our spiritual growth and development. The Redemptorists focus on the importance of fundamental conversion and the important role of prayer for the working out of our salvation.[9] "In my Father's house there are many dwelling places" (Jn 14:2). Such differences in emphasis ensure that everyone can find a place within the Church and call it home and, as Jesus' own words suggest, are perhaps a foreshadowing of an even greater diversity yet to come.

Members of these orders should be familiar with their tradition and able to make appropriate adaptations to their present situation. They should also be able to introduce others to the practice of spiritual direction within their tradition so that it remains a vital option for future generations as they seek to help others navigate the deep and, at times, turbulent waters of the spiritual life.

UNITY AND DIVERSITY

The previous indications make one point clear. The history of spiritual direction within Catholicism is one of diversity in the midst of an underlying unity. What Bernard of Clairvaux says about relations among religious orders also holds true for the approaches to spiritual direction sponsored by them:

> I admire them all. I belong to one of them by obser-
> vance, but to all of them by charity. We all need one
> another: the spiritual good which I do not own and
> possess, I receive from others....In this exile, the
> Church is still on pilgrimage and is, in a certain sense,
> plural: she is a single plurality and a plural unity. All
> our diversities, which make manifest the richness of
> God's gifts, will continue to exist in the one house of
> the Father, which has many rooms. Now there is a
> division of graces; then there will be distinctions of
> glory. Unity, both here and there consists in one and
> the same charity.[10]

Relations among the many traditions of spiritual direction within the larger tradition of the Catholic faith should not be characterized by jealously, suspicion, and competition, but by a deep bond of mutual respect and concern. They should share with one another so that they can receive from others what they do not yet own and possess. Because of their common faith, they truly belong to one another and should work to-gether to build one another up.

The same holds true for developing traditions among the laity. One of the greatest changes in the practice of spiritual direction over the past twenty-five years has been the increas-ing number of lay persons who have received training in and who offer spiritual direction to others.[11] Many of these have been trained in the tradition of a particular religious community.

Others have chosen freely from a variety of traditions to form an approach particularly suited to them and the situation in which they find themselves. Still others have banded together to develop their own approach which has all the traits of a distinctive tradition.

Today, spiritual direction in the Catholic tradition is clearly seen as a ministry to which all members of the faithful may be called—priest, religious, and lay. Relations among them and the great variety of traditions they represent should be marked by a celebration of the "single plurality" and "plural unity" that makes them such a rich asset of the Church's spiritual life.

A SPIRITUALITY OF COMMUNION

In his recent apostolic letter, *Novo millennio ineunte* ("At the Beginning of the New Millennium"), Pope John Paul II presents this challenge by emphasizing the importance of living a spirituality of communion. His description of this approach to life in Christ has great relevance for understanding the underlying goal of spiritual direction in the Catholic tradition:

> A spirituality of communion indicates above all the heart's contemplation of the mystery of the Trinity in us, and whose light we must also be able to see shining on the face of the brothers and sisters around us. A spirituality of communion also means an ability to think of our brothers and sisters in faith within the profound unity of the Mystical Body, and therefore as "those who are a part of me." This makes us able to share their joys and sufferings, to sense their desires and attend to their needs, to offer them deep and genuine friendship. A spirituality of communion implies also the ability to see what is positive in others, to welcome it and prize it as a gift from God: not only as a gift for the brother or sister who has received it directly,

but also as a "gift for me." A spirituality of communion means, finally, to know how to "make room" for our brothers and sisters, bearing "each other's burdens" (Gal 6:2) and resisting the selfish temptations which constantly beset us and provoke competition, careerism, distrust, and jealously. Let us have no illusions: unless we follow this spiritual path, external structures of communion will serve very little purpose. They will become mechanisms without a soul, "masks" of communion rather than its means of expression and growth.[12]

When applied to spiritual direction, these words remind directors that the inner relations of the Trinity should be transposed onto their own relationships with those they seek to serve.[13] Christ's mystical body is a celebration of the deep intimate communion between God and humanity. It propels directors to go out to others, to dialogue with them, and to establish deep bonds of friendship. It also calls them to unmask any false structures or ways of relating that keep those they minister to from living in communion with themselves, others, and God.

The pope's words should inspire spiritual directors to establish a spirituality of communion within their own ranks. They can do this first and foremost by building bonds of unity among the various traditions of spiritual guidance within the Catholic faith. They can then seek to establish bonds of communion with traditions of spiritual guidance within other Christian churches and then among those from non-Christian religions. The goal is to recognize positive points of correlation with other spiritual traditions and use them as starting points for dialogue and ongoing cooperation. Enriched by other traditions of spiritual guidance, directors will ultimately come to a better understanding and more profound appreciation of their own.

The primary criterion for determining the worth of a particular tradition of spiritual guidance is whether it succeeds in helping individuals to establish deep, lasting bonds of communion with themselves, others, and God. These relationships should be concrete, easy to identify, and evident in the way individuals and groups interact with one another. Specific practices used by directors to foster such bonds should not harbor any underlying prejudices that unknowingly provoke competition, careerism, distrust, and jealously.

OBSERVATIONS

Christian spiritual direction as a communion of traditions asks directors to celebrate their unity of purpose in the midst of their diversity of approaches. The following remarks offer some suggestions about what such a celebration might entail.

1. The word *tradition* is here taken in the common dictionary sense of "a body of beliefs and usages handed down from generation to generation."[14] This implies elements of both theory and practice and a way of passing them on to others through time. Those standing within a particular tradition of spiritual direction have the primary responsibility of elucidating the nature of these various beliefs and usages. Those responsible should be particularly interested in developing flexible structures that will be able to adapt the insights of their tradition in an appropriate way to changing historical circumstances.

2. The word *communion* means "sharing in an intimate way."[15] This understanding of the word implies different degrees of communion. Since intimacy is not something that can be forced, it also requires a free, reciprocal participation by the various parties involved. To speak of spiritual direction in terms of a communion of traditions implies that people adhering to those traditions see the value of sharing their own riches of spiritual insights in order to be enriched by those of others. It implies a recognition that no tradition of spiritual direction

is so complete that it cannot learn from and be deepened by contact with another.

3. The phrase *communion of traditions* requires a look to the past, present, and future. It asks those participating in it to cast off whatever suspicion or distrust may have influenced the interaction of their traditions in the past. It asks them to seize the present moment so that they may engage in a genuine and mutually enriching dialogue. It asks them to look forward with hope that each tradition of direction may be empowered to become more and more what it is called to be.

4. A communion of traditions has nothing to do with sameness or homogeneity. Rather than a watering down of a director's knowledge of his or her own tradition, it requires a deeper probing of what that tradition stands for. It is impossible to share what one does not possess nor has little knowledge of. Because a communion of traditions involves sharing one's tradition in an intimate way with another, it presupposes that the director has taken the time to appropriate his or her own tradition. Otherwise, what is being shared is never truly one's own.

5. Directors appropriate their tradition by supervised practice. Theoretical knowledge is necessary, but only goes so far. Reading about what the practice of spiritual direction within one's tradition entails can only introduce a person to the subtleties of a particular tradition. Appropriating a tradition of spiritual direction means having firsthand knowledge and then reflecting upon that knowledge with the help of a recognized teacher. In spiritual direction, theory without supervised practice would be like going to a doctor who has read the medical books, but who has never had an internship or residency.

6. This communion of traditions also requires spiritual directors to be conscious of the various levels of spirituality itself: the experiential, the doctrinal, and the analytical.[16] A genuine communion of traditions requires a willingness to look at one's experience of communion, to develop some sort of

teaching regarding it, and then subject these first two levels to careful analysis. Only in this way will it comply with the fundamental requisites of spirituality in general, let alone the more particularized requirements of a spirituality of communion.

7. *Spirituality* itself can be defined as "what we do with our deepest yearnings."[17] When applied to a spirituality of communion and its application to spiritual direction as a community of traditions, it means sharing intimately within ourselves, with others who share our tradition, and in varying degrees of intensity with directors from other traditions. In the latter case, those closest to one's own tradition deserve priority of place. One should then work outward, as if in concentric circles, with those increasingly less similar to one's own.[18]

8. When directors employ such a model of concentric circles to understand in a rough, diagrammatic sense the movement of their attempts at communion, they should be aware that their own tradition may be placed on the periphery (the outer circle, if you will) of another's plan. No single tradition has a monopoly on perspective. The hard work of dialogue involves being faithful to one's own perspective, while at the same time respecting that of one's partners. To take full advantage of this approach, directors must be comfortable enough with their own tradition that they can admit its weaknesses and recognize that it can be enriched (and perhaps even developed) by insights from another.

9. Still, participating in a communion of traditions requires a point of view. Those who, for whatever reason, do not identify themselves with a particular tradition of spiritual direction should be encouraged to examine the approach they take to their ministry and determine which of the many traditions they have been exposed to is most sympathetic to their own beliefs. Entering into sympathy with that tradition will enrich their ministry and provide them with an important touchstone for experiencing and evaluating others that they encounter along the way.

10. Finally, those participating in a communion of traditions should be encouraged to practice that kind of healthy eclecticism which combs through other traditions for what can be of genuine use to them in their own. Such spiritual directors pick and choose not in an erratic, aimless manner, but with the specific purpose of finding valid points of convergence between their own tradition of direction and others with which they come in contact. Such a practice expands the director's horizons and may eventually make a valuable contribution to the development of his or her tradition.

These are just some of the practical ways in which directors can participate in a genuine communion of traditions. Doing so will enable them to appreciate their own tradition even more and inspire them to seek even greater ways of sharing their own insights into their tradition with others.

CONCLUSION

The history of spiritual direction contains a variety of traditions, each of which has made valuable contributions to the current understanding and practice of the ministry. In this chapter we have outlined some of the important streams of influence that have been involved in shaping the historical flow of the discipline on the level of both theory and practice. We have also emphasized the need for spiritual directors to name the particular tradition to which they belong and to take ownership of it. Only then will they be in a position to share the various beliefs and practices that make up that tradition with others in an intimate way.

Living a spirituality of communion means many things. For spiritual directors it involves seeking to forge a genuine communion of traditions that will make the ministry of spiritual accompaniment an experience of single plurality and plural unity. This unity in diversity must steer clear of the extremes of homogeneity and relativism. It should celebrate one's

13

rootedness in a particular tradition, while also encouraging directors to explore new ways in which their own traditions can develop.

Spiritual directors are called to be in the forefront of efforts to foster a communion of traditions within their ministry. They can do so through critical reflection on their own tradition and honest sharing with those who are seriously interested in deepening their own understanding of the movement of the Spirit in people's lives.

REFLECTION QUESTIONS

1. Which stream of Christian spiritual direction has influenced you the most? the Roman Catholic? the Protestant? the Orthodox? Which are you most familiar with? Which are you least familiar with? Which do you feel most drawn to? Which do you feel most distant from? Have you made any attempt to dialogue with those traditions less familiar to you?

2. Are you familiar with the variety of approaches to spiritual direction within the Catholic tradition? If so, how would you describe them? Which do you feel most drawn to? What strengths do you find in such variety? Are there any weaknesses? Do these approaches complement each other in any way?

3. Which tradition of spiritual direction do you identify with the most? Why do you identify with it? How do you do so? Why is it important to be able to name and take ownership of the tradition to which one belongs? Are there other traditions that have influenced you to some degree? To what degree have you been able to name and take ownership of them?

4. What does living a "spirituality of communion" mean to you? Is this an abstract notion or something you have already experienced? Do you think it can be applied to the

ministry of spiritual direction? If so, how? If not, why not? What advantages would spiritual directors gain from such an approach? Does it present any dangers or possible disadvantages?

5. Are you comfortable with the spiritual tradition to which you belong? Are you proud of it? ashamed of it? Do you have mixed feelings about it? Do you know what distinguishes it from other traditions? How do you understand the ministry of spiritual direction within that tradition? What can it contribute to other approaches to direction? How can it benefit from them?

Chapter Two

SAINT ALPHONSUS: SPIRITUAL MASTER

W hen dealing with the life and works of Alphonsus de Liguori, we cannot expect to find precise, ready-made solutions for how the practice of spiritual direction should be conducted today. It would equally be unrealistic, however, to think that he has nothing at all to offer our current understanding of the ministry. Although Alphonsus was limited by the general spiritual outlook of his day, he was also at times both probing and creative enough to surpass it—and often with great benefit to the people he served. In understanding Alphonsus's relevance for spiritual direction today, much will depend on how we approach his thought and which aspect of it we choose to emphasize. In this chapter, we will examine the basis of his reputation as a spiritual master and identify those elements that can be helpful to those who are interested in using the Alphonsian perspective as a touchstone for their practice of spiritual direction.

A Gospel Spirituality

At the very outset, it is important for us to recognize Alphonsus's deep missionary fervor. The major projects of his life—his mission preaching, his writing, the work of founding the Redemptorist Congregation, his life of prayer—were all motivated by his profound desire to share the Good News of plentiful redemption in Christ with others, especially the poor and most abandoned. Alphonsian spirituality is first and foremost a Gospel spirituality, one rooted in the person of Jesus Christ and which takes seriously the Lord's injunction to his apostles to "make disciples of all nations" (Mt 28:19). In the context of eighteenth-century Naples, Alphonsus interpreted this calling (and personalized it) in a very specific way. Rather than looking to the foreign missions, he looked to those areas in his own backyard where people did not have easy access to the ordinary means provided by the Church for spiritual growth.

This option for the poor and willingness to go where others refused to travel led Alphonsus and his small band of followers to the hilltops and small mountain villages on the back roads of the kingdom of Naples. Their evangelizing efforts for the poor, illiterate peasant stock they found in the forgotten hamlets of Campania, Puglia, Basilicata, and Calabria helped change the spiritual landscape of southern Italy. These early Redemptorist missioners reminded those they served that God had not forgotten them, but was very much with them in their desire and thirst for spiritual growth. To ensure that such growth would continue, Alphonsus and his followers set up flexible structures of devotional practice (for example, confraternities, eucharistic devotions, evening chapels) that would help to foster a life of prayer and devotion in these fledgling faith communities once they had left.

Alphonsus's particular brand of Gospel spirituality helps us to appreciate even more the various nuances in the old debate about whether there is a single Christian spirituality—or many.[1] To the extent that every expression of it must be rooted in the person of Christ, Christian spirituality is fundamentally one. At various times in the Church's history, however, certain individuals and groups have been called to root their following of Christ in a particular work, spiritual practice, or style of living. The great number of religious congregations, secular institutes, and lay movements that have appeared in the history of the Church point to the almost infinite number of expressions that can be given to the following of Christ. In this sense, there are many Christian spiritualities—and many still to come. For our present purposes, Alphonsus's own way of practicing the love of Jesus Christ can be thought of as being both different from and united to all other authentic Christian spiritualities. Because of its flexibility and popular diffusion, moreover, his particular brand of Gospel spirituality reminds us that the term spirituality itself allows for various nuances and can be treated on a number of levels.[2]

A MAN OF PRAYER

Throughout his life, Alphonsus's overriding purpose was to do all he could to draw others closer to Christ. He believed that everyone could share an intimate relationship with Jesus and that the key to developing such a relationship was to be persistent and dedicated in the life of prayer. "He who prays is certainly saved. He who prays not is certainly damned."[3] These words of Alphonsus indicate the strong emphasis that he placed on the role of prayer in fostering a mature relationship with God.

Prayer, for Alphonsus, was "the great means of salvation."[4] Everyone, he believed, received sufficient grace to pray. *Meditatio*, or mental prayer, was particularly important for turning one's whole heart and mind to the Lord.[5] Alphonsus, in fact, would develop a very easy formula of mental prayer that could be easily taught to the simple rustics of the Italian hill country. He simplified this prayer form and thus introduced them to one of the great riches of the Church's spiritual tradition. In doing so, he was heavily criticized by a number of enlightened Neapolitan clerics for casting pearls to swine, and thereby desecrating the Church's treasures by sharing them with people who could not possibly appreciate them, let alone put them into practice.

Alphonsus, however, had little time for such judgmental remarks (or for those who made them). Throughout his life, he pursued a consistent policy of popularizing the Church's teaching on prayer in a simple, easily understandable style. He met people where they were and helped them, little by little, to pray to God as intimate friends speak to one another. "Paradise for God…is the human heart," he liked to say.[6] Prayer, for Alphonsus, was the means *par excellence* for enabling this divine indwelling to occur. He never tired of emphasizing the centrality of prayer for the spiritual life, "There may be some who, after the perusal of my spiritual works, will accuse me of tediousness in so often recommending the importance and necessity of having continual recourse to God in prayer. But I seem to myself to have said not too much, but far too little."[7] Not only did he emphasize this central theme in his own writings, but he also encouraged others to do the same, "…I say, and repeat, and will keep on repeating as long as I live, that our whole salvation depends on prayer; and therefore, that all writers in their books, all preachers in their sermons, all confessors in their instructions to their penitents, should not inculcate anything more strongly than continual prayer."[8] It is no small coincidence that Alphonsus is often referred to as the Doctor of Prayer.[9] Prayer was the centerpiece of his spiritual doctrine. For him, we can get nowhere in the spiritual life without it. With it, we have access to the copious redemption made possible for us through the passion, death, and resurrection of Jesus Christ.

AN ARRAY OF INFLUENCES

Alphonsus's profound interest in prayer did not develop in a vacuum. He first learned to pray at home. As with most families of eighteenth-century Naples, the Liguori family life was organized externally by his father and internally by his mother. The former took charge of upholding the family's name, conducting its business affairs, and developing strong relations—both religious and social—within the kingdom. The latter nurtured the family's inner affective life and was the major presence in its day-to-day functioning.[10] As the eldest son and firstborn of seven children, Alphonsus bore on his shoulders the weight of his parents' deepest aspirations. His father, Don Giuseppe, was a captain in the Royal Navy and carried home to his family the strong disciplinary manner that he often used on ship. His mother, Donna Anna Cavalieri, was a sensitive woman who led an intensely passionate life of prayer that she carefully tried to impart to her children. Both parents had a profound impression on Alphonsus. His father's harshness and long absences from home created a certain distance (one might almost say a reverential fear) in Alphonsus's attitude and bearing toward authority. Donna Anna, by way of contrast, led an austere life that some might say was more befitting of a cloistered nun (which she had always desired to become) than a mother of seven. Her motherly affection was intimately bound up with her life of prayer, and she communicated that sense of the spiritual to her children very well. These primary parental characteristics—discipline, austerity, and passionate prayer—were impressed on Alphonsus from an early age and had a major impact on the development of his character. They stayed with him throughout his life and colored much of the way he viewed his relationships to God and others. They would also color his understanding of religious life, especially in his interpretation of the vows.[11]

In addition to what he received from his family, Alphonsus's understanding of the way to holiness was also influenced by many of the great schools of Christian spirituality. He was exposed to these through his own avid study and spiritual reading and also through membership in a number of sodalities that organized retreats, spiritual exercises, and charitable activities among the nobility of Naples.[12] Even a cursory reading of his voluminous literary output shows that Alphonsus was extremely well-read in the Scriptures, the Fathers of the Church, and the great spiritual masters of the Western Church.[13] Of all that he was exposed to, four streams of spirituality, in particular, had a profound effect on his spiritual outlook. Like Saint Teresa of Ávila (1515–82), one of the patrons of his religious institute, he saw the importance of practical realism, a deep sacramental sense, dogmatic orthodoxy, and a strong Catholic identity. With Saint Ignatius of Loyola (1491–1556), he emphasized a spirit of service based on effective, prudential love for the common good. Like Saint Francis de Sales (1567–1622), he stressed the abundance and gratuity of salvation, the tenderness of God's love, and conformity to the divine will. Like him, Alphonsus also highlighted the importance of ejaculatory prayer for personal recollection, of developing a popular lay spirituality, and of learning and the arts as important aids to holiness. Finally, with the Oratorians of Naples, whom he met through their General, Matteo Ripa (1682–1746), he emphasized such themes as participation in the Divine Image, the centrality of the Trinity, Grace, and a devotional life based on the Incarnation and the Eucharist. Through this same influence, he demonstrated an interest in the theology of states of life within the Church, and highlighted the simplicity, discipline, and training needed for an authentic spirituality of Christian childhood.[14] In keeping with his highly focused and pragmatic spiritual ends, Alphonsus borrowed from these schools in a creatively eclectic way to create his own synthesis that was relevant to his particular mission in the Church, that is, to preach the Gospel to the poor and most abandoned.[15]

Throughout his writing, Alphonsus quoted these and many other spiritual authors with a twofold purpose in mind. In the first place, he believed that knowledge of their teachings would help his readers to come closer to Christ. In the second place, he wished to steep them in the rich spiritual tradition of the Church. For Alphonsus, the two aims were obviously connected. Deeply aware of his own limitations as a spiritual writer, he immersed himself in the lives and mystical writings of the saints in order to nourish himself and also those he preached to and wrote for. By presenting his readers with examples from their lives and teachings, he firmly believed that they would have before them all that was necessary for walking the path of holiness. Of all the saints mentioned in his writings, Alphonsus gave special prominence to the Blessed Mother. Her humble *fiat* enabled her to play a special role in God's plan of redemption. As a result, Alphonsus considered her intercession with her son on our behalf especially important. "To Jesus through Mary," he liked to say. Mary, in his mind, mediated all graces to us from her son and ultimately would lead us to him.[16]

ON LEADING OTHERS TO GOD

Leading others to Christ is what Alphonsus's missionary vocation was all about. This profound conviction helps to explain his deep Marian piety. Mary's vocation and her role in the Church centered on this same fundamental calling. By staying close to Mary, Alphonsus felt reassured that his own vocation of leading others to her son would intensify and bear much fruit. This sensibility explains why his writings are full of theological references, edifying stories, and heartfelt prayers to the Madonna. Mary, who pondered in her heart all that happened to her son, is the Christian disciple *par excellence*. In his own efforts to follow Christ and to contemplate the great events of the Paschal Mystery, Alphonsus greatly relied on Mary's generous help and protection.[17]

We have already seen how, when taken under the general heading of the "care and cure of souls," spiritual direction encompasses virtually every aspect of the Church's pastoral ministry. Such an assessment would be doubly true for someone like Alphonsus, who labored assiduously through his preaching, writing, direction of souls, and general pastoral care to do all he could to lead others to a deeper and more intimate relationship with God. When taken in this general sense, everything that Alphonsus did can be considered a kind of spiritual direction. Even those activities which did not directly touch the lives of the people he served (for example, his prayer, spiritual reading, his own private devotions) had an underlying missionary dimension to them. It should not be surprising that these same activities often had an underlying (and often very visible) Marian dimension to them as well. What is more, the subtle balance between contemplation and action that characterized Mary's joyful *fiat* are characteristic of Alphonsus's approach to his missionary activity. For Alphonsus, prayer and action are two sides of the same apostolic coin. To separate them or to give undue precedence to one could run the risk of doing grave damage to both the missionary and the people he has been called upon to serve.

When taken in the more specific sense of "a helping relationship focusing on a person's growth in the spiritual life," Alphonsus's approach to spiritual direction is directive in nature and closely tied to his confessional practice. That is not to say that he did not, at times, resort to spiritual direction through correspondence or that he never conducted a session of spiritual direction outside of the confessional.[18] On the contrary, his practical temperament and his eclectic use of the Church's spiritual tradition led him to take attenuating circumstances into account and to adapt his pastoral praxis to the cases at hand. In general, however, Alphonsus saw a close connection between spiritual direction and sacramental confession. While he was aware of the distinction between the two, he was very firm in

his insistence that the confessor be someone who not only for-
gives sins, but who can also lead the penitent further along the
path of sanctity.[19]

Alphonsus's strong penchant for uniting the two appear
most clearly in his *Praxis confessarii*, where he delineates in
descending hierarchical order the four offices of the confessor
to be those of father, doctor, teacher, and judge.[20] For
Alphonsus, every confessor had the responsibility of guiding
souls to sanctity. This was so because all the faithful (not just
a select few) were called to the perfection of Christian living.
The term spiritual director, in other words, was not set aside
simply for those who guided people through the rarified states
of mystical experience, but for all confessors who helped men
and women from various states of life within the Church to
walk the path of holiness. When seen in this light, Alphonsus
went a long way in demystifying the role of spiritual director
in the Christian tradition. His strong popularizing efforts
brought the riches of the spiritual life to the person in the pew.
This meat-and-potatoes approach to the spiritual life was a
benchmark of Redemptorist practice and characterized the
Alphonsian approach to direction for years to come.

More specifically, the principal characteristics of the
Alphonsian confessor-director were:

1. An attitude of being more of a father and doctor
   than a judge. This attitude manifested itself in the
   charity, goodness, and mildness with which one
   welcomed and treated the penitent and in the task
   of disposing him or her to penitence so that one
   would not feel obligated to defer or to deny abso-
   lution.

2. An attitude of kindness in giving penance, seeking
   more that would heal the soul than the punishment or satisfaction for the fault committed.

3. A marked preference for the poorest and most ignorant of the social classes.

4. A concern for giving the penitent not only the means of perseverance for preventing a relapse into sin but also for giving the means for advancing in the way of holiness.

5. Recognizing the relationship between preaching and confession: preaching prepares the way for confession and continues the work undertaken by it.[21]

These characteristics of the Alphonsian confessor-director demonstrate the practical orientation of Alphonsus's mission. He sought to preach the good news of plentiful redemption to as many people as possible. In this capacity, he saw the wisdom of treating the confessional not as a tribunal, but as a means for educating the faithful in the ways of holiness. The intrinsic connection that he saw between preaching and confession also reveal that he himself understood the direction process as something that extended to the ordinary care of souls.

It should also be stated that, confined as he was by the theological outlook of the post-Tridentine Church of eighteenth-century Naples, Alphonsus sought in his own way to preserve a certain communion of the various spiritual traditions in the Church. Ecumenical and interreligious dialogue was not a viable option in his day. There was still too much polemic and mutual antagonism among the various Christian denominations for constructive dialogue to take place, and the Church's primary stance toward members of non-Christian faith was characterized by a twofold strategy of outright condemnation of their religious tenets accompanied by the call to conversion. In Western Christianity, moreover, the Church had to struggle against the ongoing threats of Protestant proselytism, Janenist rigorism, Quietist laxism, and the strong secularizing tendencies of Enlightenment thought. In dealing with such threats, the Church adopted a defensive, fortress mentality that tried to shelter the faithful from as many dangerous and harmful influences as possible. It should not be surprising that Alphonsus, a loyal son of the Church, espoused similar views and, as such, was thoroughly conditioned by the times in which he lived.

With regard to spiritual traditions within the Church, however, Alphonsus displays a remarkable openness to the variety of approaches that he encountered. Once the critical test of orthodoxy had been passed, he felt free to borrow whatever he thought might be useful to him in his mission of bringing about a fundamental conversion or change of heart in the lives of the people he ministered to, especially the poor and most abandoned. This pragmatic openness to other spiritual traditions stood in marked contrast to the quarrelsome (and often petty) arguments that went on among many of the religious orders of his day. Such unhealthy competitiveness focused on the small points that separated their approaches to the spiritual life, rather than what united them. Alphonsus much preferred to concentrate on what bound them together. His key rule of thumb in that regard was whether or not a particular spiritual practice drew people closer to Christ. A second corollary was that it be beneficial to as many people as possible. This practical eclecticism led him to a synthetic approach to direction that was peculiarly his own. To cite just one example, he valued highly the spiritual doctrine of Teresa of Ávila on the interior mansions of infused contemplation and encouraged directors to follow it whenever they encountered someone who exhibited tendencies toward such mystical states. Unlike some representatives of the Carmelite school of spirituality, however, he affirmed with the Jesuits that not everyone was called to infused contemplation in this life and therefore focused his efforts in the direction of souls in the areas of meditation and acquired contemplation.[22]

In the final analysis, Alphonsus was convinced that it was

not a method or a particular approach to the spiritual life that led people to *metanoia* or a change of heart, but a personal encounter with Jesus Christ. To this end, Alphonsus probed a variety of spiritual traditions within the Church and used whatever he thought would be beneficial to the people he served. Doing so, for Alphonsus, was an exercise of Christian love. In this respect, he would have wholeheartedly agreed with Bernard of Clairvaux's assessment of the variety of families of spirituality in the Church, "I admire them all. I belong to one of them by observance, but to all of them by charity."[23]

CONCLUSION

As mentioned earlier, Alphonsus's reputation as a spiritual master eventually earned him the title Doctor of Prayer.[24] His renown as a spiritual director comes from his creative, eclectic, and pragmatic use of the traditions that preceded him. As an interpreter of these traditions, he focused on the one thing which, in his judgment, ultimately mattered in life: to enter into an intimate relationship with Jesus, the Redeemer. Prayer, for Alphonsus, was the primary means given to us to accomplish this end. Spiritual direction, for him, was both general and particular. It could take place in many contexts, but primarily had to do with the confessor's task of helping a person to grow in holiness.

While Alphonsus saw a distinction between the confession and spiritual direction, his pragmatic orientation, zeal for souls, and deep popularizing sensitivities brought him to the prudential conclusion that in his day and age the people of God could best be served by drawing a close bond between the two. Sacramental confession, after all, was an application of Christ's redemptive love to the life of the penitent. Since redemption was plentiful, for Alphonsus, it followed that the experience of sacramental reconciliation should include not only the forgiveness of sin but also concrete guidance that would enable the penitent to grow in holiness. He believed that spiritual direction was for the masses—not a select few—and for people of all walks of life. The close bond that he saw between preaching and the confession-spiritual direction experience also points to the organic (even circular) relationship between the general and more particular elements of the direction process.

These considerations have great importance for those who are trying to understand the relevance of Alphonsus's spiritual doctrine for today. His walk with the Lord was, at one and the same time, both similar to and different from our own. Walking in his footsteps today cannot possibly mean following his teachings to the letter. Such an approach would overlook the prudential nature of Alphonsus's own pastoral decisions and fail to take into account the pressing concerns and very different pastoral needs of our own historical circumstances.

On the contrary, following Alphonsus today means being willing to make a creative, eclectic, and pragmatic use of the spiritual traditions that have preceded us—especially that of Alphonsus himself. It means sifting through the various teachings and practices that he himself considered beneficial for the people of his day and trying to find appropriate practical parallels for our own times. For our present purposes, it means trying to develop an approach to spiritual direction that will give people easy access to the liberating message of the plentiful redemption of Christ and helping to foster an ongoing conversation with God in the deepest recesses of their hearts. Spiritual direction in the Alphonsian tradition today should not pretend to be an exact replica of what it was during Alphonsus's lifetime—or even try. It should resonate with his teaching, however, and be clearly seen as something that flows from his zealous missionary spirit and his deep desire to lead as many people as possible into a deep intimate friendship with the Lord.

REFLECTION QUESTIONS

1. Do you identify with Alphonsus's Gospel spirituality? What do you find attractive about it? What is difficult about it? How can it be translated into the cultural setting in which you find yourself? Who are the poor and most abandoned in your midst? How would Alphonsus reach out to them?

2. Why was prayer so important for Alphonsus? Why was it for him "the great means of salvation"? Do you feel the same way about prayer as he did? Is it a central element of your life? Can you live without it? Do you speak to God as one intimate friend speaks to another? What do you tell God? What does God say to you?

3. There were many influences that shaped Alphonsus's spiritual outlook. What are the major influences on yours? Can you identify them quickly and with little trouble? Does it take some thought? Do you think there may be some influences on your spiritual outlook of which you might not be fully aware? How might you go about trying to get in touch with them?

4. Do you find Alphonsus's "creative eclecticism" attractive? What strengths does this approach to the spiritual traditions of the Church have? Can you see any weaknesses in it? Are you "creatively eclectic" in your approach to spirituality? If so, how? If not, then how *would* you describe your approach?

5. Do you agree with the main characteristics of Alphonsus's approach to confession and spiritual direction? Do you believe they are just as applicable today as they were in Alphonsus's day? What elements can be directly translated into the present day? What elements might need to be adapted?

Chapter Three

SAINT ALPHONSUS AND PRAYER

W ith its close ties to sacramental reconciliation, Alphonsus's compassionate, yet highly directive approach to spiritual direction greatly influenced the Catholic thought of its day and would do so for many years to come. For a variety of reasons, however, it gradually fell out of sync with the way the ministry developed in the post-Vatican II era. Unlike Alphonsus, most of today's directors employ an approach of nondirective, nonsacramental spiritual accompaniment.[1] Although this model does not entirely disallow the more directive approach of the kind used by Alphonsus, it places much more emphasis on enabling the person receiving direction to discern for himself or herself the next steps that need to be taken on his or her spiritual journey. In this chapter, we will try to determine if anything in the Alphonsian tradition might help us to respond to this recent shift in emphasis.

THE GRADES OF PRAYER

Since the conversation involved in spiritual accompaniment usually focuses on a person's prayer life, a good place to begin would be Alphonsus's own understanding of and judgments concerning the various grades of prayer. Here, he recognized the classical distinctions between *oratio* (that is, vocal prayer), *meditatio* (that is, meditation or mental prayer), and *contemplatio* (that is, contemplation).[2] To capture the various nuances between these fundamental "types," he generally follows the teaching of Teresa of Ávila, making only some slight adjustments for his pressing pastoral concerns. Alphonsus's teaching on prayer can be best understood against this important Teresian backdrop. According to this teaching, there are nine different grades of prayer.[3]

1. *Vocal prayer* uses words to express our hearts and minds to God. It can follow prescribed formulas as in the *Lord's Prayer* and the *Hail Mary* or be a spontaneous outpouring of the heart. It can be done in private or in a group. It also plays an important role in liturgical prayer. Because it is simple and easy to learn, it is usually the first kind of prayer to which people are introduced. Vocal prayer is embodied prayer. Through it, a person makes use of the body as a way of giving honor and glory to God. The greatest strength of vocal prayer is the way it can involve the whole person (that is, body, mind, and spirit) in prayer. It's greatest weakness is the way it can degenerate into a mechanized, external display that is void of inner meaning. Vocal prayer is important at every stage of the spiritual life. Even though it is simple and easy to learn, it should in no way be denigrated. Jesus himself encouraged his disciples to pray with heartfelt words from the heart when addressing their Father in heaven (Mt 6:7–13).

2. *Mental prayer or meditation*, for Teresa, is "nothing but friendly intercourse, and frequent solitary converse, with him who we know loves us."[4] It is a discursive type of prayer that focuses the mind on a particular gospel story or mystery of the faith. Through it, a person probes the meaning of a particular belief and makes it an integral part of his or her life. It is practiced in silence and normally for an extended time

(twenty minutes to a half an hour). It can be done both privately and in common. There are many methods of mental prayer. Most of them include a period of preparation, some reflection on a particular aspect of the faith, an application of that reflection to one's life, a resolution to do something about it, and a concluding prayer. Through mental prayer, a person is able to consider in-depth the meaning of his or her faith. When practiced regularly, it enables one to delve beneath the surface of one's beliefs and to participate with more awareness in the ongoing conversion of life.

3. *Affective prayer* brings meditation from the level of the head to that of the heart.[5] In this respect, it is merely a deeper kind of meditation. What has begun as a sustained reflection on a particular aspect of the faith gradually begins to penetrate a person's will and to manifest itself in heartfelt prayers of love and affection. In affective prayer, a person's will functions as the predominant faculty. However, since both reason and will must be present in any genuine act of mental prayer, what we are really talking about here is a matter of emphasis. At this stage, the person praying has become so absorbed in the object he or she is meditating upon that deep sentiments and inner longings of love for God swell up within the heart and find expression. Affective prayer is mental prayer that has come to term. It is the prayer of mind and heart, but with the heart playing the dominant role. Such prayer must be spontaneous and should not be forced. It is to be judged by the fruits it produces in a person's life and not by the sensible consolation that often accompanies it.

4. *Acquired recollection (also "the prayer of simplicity" or "acquired contemplation")* is a simple, loving gaze upon a concrete representation of the divine (for example, an icon, the tabernacle, the consecrated host). As such, it moves beyond the discursive level of prayer that involves the deliberated movement of the intellect and the will in mental prayer. This grade of prayer is the dividing line between the ascetical

and mystical stages of the spiritual life. During it, the person at prayer acts under the influence of grace but is still the primary agent involved in the action. This form of prayer subsumes all the fruits of mental and affective prayer into itself. Unlike these earlier forms of prayer, however, there is no specific "method" or way of going about it. It simply happens. In this prayer, one's spirit has become awakened to the divine and is content with doing nothing else but sitting in its presence. A person who prays in this way leads a simple life and shows visible signs of steady progress in the life of conversion.

5. *Infused contemplation* marks the beginning of mystical prayer in the life of the believer. Here, the person praying receives an intimate, experiential knowledge of God. This knowledge comes in the form of an intellectual light that illumines the mind and enables the person to have an intuitive, connatural knowledge of the divine. Infused contemplation is a pure gift from God. The person praying can do nothing to instigate its coming or to prolong its stay. At this stage of prayer, the person praying opens his or her mind to God in a vulnerable stance of passive receptiveness. Being open in this way to the illuminating light of the divine is itself a special gift from God and given to those especially chosen for it. Those blessed with the experience of infused contemplation receive an obscure but assured knowledge of the divine and are given the moral certitude that they are in the state of grace. They are moved to devote themselves more deeply to the interior life and normally need to place themselves under the care of a holy, learned, and experienced director.

6. *The prayer of quiet* takes the person praying into an even deeper experience of God. Whereas infused contemplation fills the intellect with the illuminating light of the divine, the prayer of quiet allows that light to penetrate the will. The result is an experience of intense joy and inner consolation. At this stage, the will is captivated and totally absorbed in God. The person praying in this way is given great freedom of spirit,

a filial respect and deep confidence in God, a love of suffering, uncommon humility, detachment from worldly pleasures, and the desire to grow in the virtues. At this level, it is normally very difficult for the person to describe his or her experiences of God. As the name suggests, the person blessed with this experience tends toward solitude and repose, but is able to actively engage the other faculties of the soul. The experience of quiet may last for a long time or for only a few moments. The person who receives this experience should be grateful when it occurs and, when it passes, should be encouraged to continue to pray in other ways.

7. *The prayer of union* brings the person praying to an even deeper experience of the divine. In the prior two stages of contemplation only the intellect and will are captivated by the illuminating light of God. Here, all the internal faculties also become absorbed in this intense penetrating light. The memory and imagination are particularly affected at this stage. They become totally focused on God and, as a result, leave the person praying free of all distractions and weariness. Those blessed with this experience are certain of their intimate union with God. They experience him with such intensity that they can easily become "beside themselves" by falling into ecstasy. Being absorbed in God in this way can last for but a few fleeting moments or for hours. During such times, the person can sometime feel a sensible "touch," an intense "fiery dart" or a longer lasting "wound of love" in the soul. These experiences are not essential to the prayer of union, but are often associated with it. They reveal the heights of mystical experience and indicate an intense relationship of love between God and the person praying.

8. *Spiritual betrothal* occurs when the divine light captivates the soul's external senses. This stage is an extension of the prayer of union. Now, not only the internal sense but also the external senses of hearing, sight, smell, taste, and touch are distanced, either totally or in part, from their ordinary

functioning. The person's internal and external senses are so absorbed in God that he or she finds it exceedingly difficult to become involved in external activity. At this stage, mystical ecstasy (as in standing "outside of one's senses") is part and parcel of a person's experience of the divine. It can be gentle and pleasing to the person praying or intensely violent and painful. In spiritual betrothal the person praying enters into a deep covenant with God. The soul is pulled up out of its senses and becomes totally awake to the divine world. This state of betrothal or conforming union leads the soul to the threshold of perfect, mystical union with God.

9. *Spiritual marriage* brings about the total absorption of the soul into God. Although the distinction between creator and creature remains, the soul's subjective experience is such that a complete identification with the divine love has taken place. This transformation of the soul into the Beloved is permanent and involves a complete surrender of self. The person seeks God in all things and is willing to undergo the greatest of trials for the love of God. At this stage, the intense spiritual ecstasies of the previous stages greatly diminish—and even disappear. Instead, the person is blessed with a vivid awareness of God's deep, abiding love. It is here, in this inner sanctum where the person communes with the Trinity in a way that, in this life, cannot be equaled. Only the beatific vision can take the soul further into the mysterious depths of the Godhead. People who experience God in this way possess a deep spirit of detachment and have a deep desire to serve God. They put others before themselves and are willing to undergo great suffering for the coming of the kingdom.

These nine grades of prayer generally correspond to the purgative (grades one to four), the illuminative (grades five and six), and the unitive ways (grades seven through nine). It must be remembered, however, that these stages of the spiritual journey do not always occur in strict succession. More often than not, they are mingled in a person's life and are very difficult to isolate. For this reason, it is usually better to ask which of these stages is the dominant emphasis in a person's life at any particular moment and in which general direction he or she is moving, that is, toward or away from union with God. Such a determination is usually a good indication of person's spiritual state.[6]

Another way of looking at these grades of prayer is to understand them in terms of the seven spiritual mansions of Teresa's spiritual masterpiece *The Interior Castle*. Although Teresa says very little about the kind of prayer that goes on in the first three mansions, we can generally assume that the believer is slowly making progress in vocal prayer, mental prayer, affective prayer, and acquired recollection, those stages normally referred to as "the four degrees of ordinary prayer." In the fourth mansion, the believer experiences infused contemplation and the prayer of quiet; in the fifth, the prayer of union; in the sixth, spiritual betrothal; and in the seventh, spiritual marriage. The first three mansions refer to what is typically referred to as the ascetical life, while the final four mansions are concerned with the mystical.[7] The understanding that there were various levels of both the ascetical and mystical states would have been very familiar to the Catholic mind-set of the post-Tridentine era.

A BLANKETED SKY

In the light of the above, a good metaphor for understanding Alphonsus's approach to prayer is to envision a world with a sky that is blanketed by a dark, impermeable substance. Above that cloudlike covering is the realm of divine light. Below it, is the visible world we know. This divine light is not grace (be it actual or sanctifying) or the illuminating light (in the Augustinian sense) that allows us to know with certitude things around us, but the experiential knowledge of God himself (the essential characteristic of the mystical state).

For Alphonsus, all of us live our lives beneath this dark, blanketed sky. Because of our feeble natural powers, however, we are unable to see through it or beyond it. Such is the human condition. Some things are simply beyond our natural capacities—and the divine light is one of them. Because of certain stories that have been revealed to us, however, some of us believe in the realm of divine light beyond the darkened sky. Others do not. Prayer is our attempt to communicate with that light beyond the pale of darkness above us. We must remember that, for Alphonsus, our belief in this upper realm of light and our attempts to communicate with it are themselves gifts of divine grace. Left to ourselves, we would care little about what exists beyond the blanketed sky above us and would make little, if any, effort to communicate with God.

Those of us who believe, however, find ourselves drawn to that realm of divine light we have heard of but have never seen. We raise our heads to the darkened sky above and begin to pray. Prayer, for Alphonsus, is simply raising our hearts and minds to God. Most of us begin by simply talking to what lies beyond the blanketed sky above us (vocal prayer). As time goes on, we find ourselves thinking more and more about the realm of divine light and trying to imagine what it could possibly be like (mental prayer). In time, our will and emotions get involved and we find ourselves pouring out our hearts to God with affectionate expressions of love and devotion (affective prayer). Further along, we become so comfortable "keeping company with God" in this way that we simply sit in silence beneath the darkened canopy above it and gaze upon the obscure secrets it withholds from us (acquired recollection). All of these forms of prayer go on without ever experiencing the divine light itself. We converse with God intimately as with a friend and may even receive certain divine inspirations, but these are a far cry from actually experiencing the divine light itself. All during this time, faith and God's grace alone sustain us and enable us to pray as we do. We yearn for the divine light and hope one day to see it. That special gift, however, is something that God alone dispenses as he sees fit.

And then one day everything changes. Out of nowhere a tiny pinhole opens up in the blanketed sky above us and a thin ray of light begins to shine through it. This tiny pinhole is not our doing, but God's—and it is for only certain people to behold. Why God has chosen this particular point in time to reveal himself to this particular person or persons remains hidden in the depths of his infinite wisdom. Those who can see this thinnest of rays are irresistibly drawn to it. They can continue talking to the divine light, thinking about it, and expressing their love for it as before, but now they have been given the unique opportunity to directly experience it. And so they turn their eyes toward it and peer into its penetrating glare. As they do so, the divine light fills their intellects (infused contemplation) and then spills out over into their wills (the prayer of quiet). From there, it fills their internal senses, especially the memory and the imagination (the prayer of union) and then their external senses (spiritual betrothal). Finally, it pulls them out of themselves and lifts them up through the pinhole in the blanketed sky and into the realm of divine light (spiritual marriage). Their union with the divine light is so intense that it is difficult for them to discern the difference between God's will and their own. They have not become the divine light but are permeated by it.

ALPHONSIAN PRAYER

The above metaphor depicts how the various grades of prayer function in the life of the believer. It helps us to understand the difference between faith knowledge and mystical knowledge.[8] It also clearly demarcates for us the difference between the ascetical and mystical lives. As far as Alphonsus is concerned, it helps us to understand why he spent so much time teaching people the earlier grades of prayer (that is, vocal prayer, meditation, affective prayer, and acquired recollection). These forms of prayer are, in fact, the only ones that can actually be taught. The mystical grades of prayer depend entirely on God and cannot be prepared for or even expected in this life. For this very reason, Alphonsus, the great "Doctor of Prayer," devoted his time and energy to providing the poor and marginalized with those tools that would best help them to nurture an intimate friendship with God.

An important concern during Alphonsus's day was the degree of accessibility of mystical states of Teresa's spiritual doctrine, that is, whether they were meant only for a select few or for a larger segment of the faithful. Alphonsus's pastoral strategy to preach the Good News of plentiful redemption to the poor and most abandoned led him to offer a nuanced response to this question. On the one hand, he focused his efforts on those grades of prayer that were usually associated with the ascetical life (that is, vocal prayer, meditation, affective prayer, and acquired recollection). These kinds of prayer were the bread and butter of the spiritual life, and he made no apologies for the insistence with which he urged the faithful to take advantage of these indispensable means of salvation. Although Alphonsus drew a clear distinction between meditation and contemplation,[9] he also recognized that the ascetical and mystical states shared much in common and were sometimes mingled with each other in the concrete circumstances of a person's life. For this reason, he understood that there was a contemplative dimension to these earlier grades of prayer, and he was very clear that the full benefits of such prayers could be reaped only if they took place against a backdrop of solitude.[10]

When seen in this light, Alphonsus's focus on the earlier grades of prayer are understood as his intense desire to get as many people as possible off to a good start in the spiritual life. Once the proper foundation was laid, he felt sure that God's grace would supply all that was necessary for a person to experience the liberating movement of the Spirit that would eventually lead to the beatific vision itself. For Alphonsus, whether or not a person had mystical experiences in the present life was a moot point. He was primarily concerned with a person's eternal destiny, not with whether he or she was ready to breathe the rarified air of spiritual marriage. Even so, he insisted that confessors and spiritual directors be capable of guiding those who demonstrated signs of genuine mystical experience. Alphonsus wanted the members of his Congregation to be prepared for every conceivable situation. Regardless of where an individual was in the spiritual life, he wanted his confreres to meet them where they were and then offer them a little bit more.

In implementing his pastoral aims, Alphonsus was a great popularizer and synthesizer. His doctrine of prayer is actually very simple. "Everyone receives sufficient grace to pray."[11] "He who prays is certainly saved. He who prays not is certainly damned."[12] "God wishes us to speak to him with confidence and familiarity."[13] "Mental prayer is morally necessary for salvation."[14] These simple phrases represent the hallmark of his teaching and could be easily remembered by those who came to him. They also point to the main characteristics of his spiritual doctrine. Alphonsian prayer is honest, humble, passionate, eclectic, practical, spontaneous, continual, popular, devotional, and petitionary. Above all, it is simple and child-like.[15] In Alphonsus's mind, everyone might not experience the heights of mystical prayer, at least in this life. All, however, are called to a life a prayer, one which will provide them with the means of salvation and which will enable them to talk to God as one friend to another. For him, mental prayer, is the one grade of prayer that most fosters this type of relationship in the lives of the faithful. It is meant for everyone, not a select few, and for this reason is the centerpiece of his teaching on prayer.

OBSERVATIONS

The previous presentation provides us with an important back-drop against which Alphonsus's approach to prayer in general and to mental prayer in particular should be understood. It also provides us with the opportunity to register a number of important critical remarks.

1. To begin with, Alphonsus's decision to focus his spiritual doctrine on the earlier grades of prayer stems from a well thought-out pastoral strategy. He wanted to preach the Good News of plentiful redemption in Christ to as many people as possible. Focusing on the lower grades of prayer helped him to cast his net widely. It also helped him to meet people where they were and to provide them with the tools they needed to deepen their relationship with Christ. This decision did not come without criticism. Some felt he was going too far by introducing his simple country peasants to the rigors of mental prayer. Others thought his simplified methods watered down the teachings of the masters and were actually doing a disservice to the Church's apostolic mission.

2. Alphonsus's response to such criticism was to become even more zealous in his attempts to instruct the poor and the marginalized in the ways of the Spirit. He could understand that not everyone would be graced to experience the higher grades of mystical prayer. He saw no need, however, to keep the means normally associated with the ascetical life away from those who needed them most. Alphonsus's pastoral strategy did much to "demystify" these prayer forms in the popular understanding. Meditation and affective prayer, he thought, should be performed not simply by priests and religious, but by everyone who had reached the age of reason. By bringing these prayer forms out of the monastery and into the household, he enabled the laity to lay claim to valuable aids to holiness. His intention here was not to turn the laity into plainclothes religious, but to give them adequate

tools that could be adapted to suit their own situation in life.

3. This pastoral strategy of focusing on the lower grades of prayer takes nothing away from Alphonsus's reputation as a spiritual master. In fact, it actually enhances it. Alphonsus was a deep man of prayer who, at various moments of his life, had been blessed by God with intense mystical experiences. It was precisely because he understood and had experienced for himself the depths of divine love that he was able to focus on those practical steps that would be most helpful to the people he was trying to serve. Alphonsus was someone who had journeyed into the depths of God's love and came back to lead others along the same path. He realized, however, that he could only get people started in the life of prayer. For the later steps of the journey, he could only lead them to the threshold of infused contemplation. From there on in he knew that he could only entrust them to God's care.

4. As a spiritual guide, Alphonsus was keenly aware of the importance of laying a proper spiritual foundation in the lives of the people he served. To this end, he dedicated himself to teaching his people the fundamentals of prayer—and then some. That little extra something was Alphonsus's way of reminding the people he served of the plentiful redemption that God was offering them. Because the ascetical life could be considered a kind of remote preparation for the mystical life, he believed that some of those who were following his "meat and potatoes" approach to prayer might eventually be blessed with intense personal encounters of the divine light. Although he did not focus on this possibility (nor encouraged others to do so), he understood that those who lived the ascetical life would be better disposed to receiving the graces necessary for the higher grades of prayer.

5. More importantly, he knew that highlighting the importance of the earlier grades of prayer would encourage people to strive for something within their reach. In doing so, he sought

to effect in them a subtle change of heart that would lead them gently on the way of conversion. Prayer, for Alphonsus, had to bring about concrete changes in the way a person lived his or her life. It was not authentic if it did not help that person grow in virtue. He saw an intricate connection between the moral and spiritual dimensions of life. Without prayer, it was impossible for human beings to lead moral lives. Through prayer, they are empowered "to put on the mind of Christ" and to conform their lives more and more to the will of God. For Alphonsus, spirituality and morality were two sides of the same coin. To separate them or to place them in separate compartments would do a grave injustice to God, to one's neighbor, and to oneself.

6. Alphonsus constantly referred to prayer as the "great means of salvation."[16] This simple phrase provides an interesting point of correlation with the current understanding of spiritual direction as helping a person to become himself or herself in the faith.[17] The relevance of this insight should not be underestimated. Since prayer and spiritual direction are both important aids to spiritual growth, it is quite feasible to think that the processes involved in one might shed light on those of the other—and vice versa. The possibility becomes even more attractive when one realizes that spiritual direction focuses primarily on a person's relationship with God and that the way a person prays is an important indicator of the strength of that relationship.

7. When seen in this light, the best place to look in the Alphonsian tradition for a point of correlation with the current understanding of spiritual direction is in his doctrine on prayer. Since his method of mental prayer is the showpiece of his teaching, it makes sense to examine the processes involved in its proper functioning for possible application to a contemporary Alphonsian model of spiritual direction. The relevance of this insight cannot be emphasized enough. It is Alphonsus's teaching on mental prayer and not his teaching on spiritual

direction that may well provide us with the elements we need to construct a viable model of direction that will adequately address the subtle shifts in emphasis that have influenced the ministry in recent times. By examining Alphonsus's understanding of the manner of making mental prayer, it may be possible to learn something about how the process of direction itself should move and what elements of a person's way of conversing with God need to be transposed onto the relationship between the director and directee.

While not exhaustive in their scope, these observations point out a number of relevant implications of Alphonsus's doctrine of prayer. They remind us that Alphonsus, the mystic, and Alphonsus, the pastor, were one and the same person. They show us how intent he was to place prayer at the very heart of his apostolic project. They also open up some new possibilities for the Alphonsian tradition of spiritual tradition. These insights remind us that Alphonsus was first and foremost an apostle of prayer. For him, teaching others to pray was intimately connected to growth in holiness. As might be expected, much of that instruction took place during spiritual direction.

CONCLUSION

Alphonsus's doctrine of prayer was greatly influenced by his pastoral motivations. His desire to touch the poor and marginalized of society with the liberating message of Christ led him to do everything in his power to make the riches of the Church's spiritual tradition as accessible as possible. To do so, he searched the tradition for those prayer forms that would be most useful to the greatest number of people. His decision to focus his teaching on the earlier grades of prayer stems from the recognition that they could be easily taught and were also the surest way of providing the faithful with a firm spiritual foundation. These practical concerns did not lead to a watering down of the Church's spiritual tradition, but to its further development and widespread diffusion.

In his own day, Alphonsus had the reputation of being a great spiritual master and an exceptional moral-pastoral theologian. He was familiar with the intricacies of the Church's mystical tradition and had personal experiences that would place him in the company of the greatest of Christian mystics.[18] At the same time, he also had a shrewd sense of the spiritual needs of the faithful and an instinctive capacity to identify what did and did not work. This unique combination of mystic visionary and pastoral handyman enabled him to unleash in the environs of eighteenth-century Naples a popular spirituality that would extend far and wide and have a deep impact on the Catholic imagination for centuries to come. Teaching people how to pray was always a central concern of this popular spirituality. When doing so, his deepest desire was to show them how they could converse continually and familiarly with God. Mental prayer, he believed, was the simplest and most practical way of achieving this end.

Today, Alphonsus's teaching on mental prayer deserves to be studied with renewed vigor. In addition to providing us with a solid basis for fostering an intimate relationship with God, it may also give us some clues about how to correlate the spirit of Alphonsus with recent developments in the ministry of spiritual direction. To see these possible points of correlation, however, it will be necessary to explore Alphonsus's teaching on the manner of making mental prayer in more detail. Doing so will enable us to identify similarities and then make appropriate adaptations for the situation that directors presently find themselves in. It will also put us in a good position to construct together a thoroughly Alphonsian model of spiritual direction for the post-Vatican II era.

REFLECTION QUESTIONS

1. Do the nine grades of prayer offer a comprehensive treatment of the spiritual life? Do they leave anything out that would be important today? Which of them do you feel most comfortable with? Which play an important role in your way of relating to God? Which have you never experienced?

2. What is your attitude toward vocal prayer? Do you look upon it as a gift or burden? What are its advantages and disadvantages? Do you pray that way often? Do you look forward to praying that way? Do you look down upon it? What is your favorite vocal prayer? Do you know why it is? Do you prefer praying it alone or in a group?

3. Do you understand the difference between meditation and affective prayer? Which do you find easier? Why do you think affective prayer is considered a deeper, more intense form of meditation? Do you think Alphonsus was right in emphasizing these grades of prayers in his pastoral strategy over the higher grades of prayer? Do you think he would do so today?

4. Do you understand the difference between acquired and infused contemplation? Who or what brings them about? How are they related? Does one necessarily lead to the other? Is everyone called to mystical prayer? In this life? In the next? What is the difference between mystical prayer and the beatific vision?

5. Do you think the later grades of prayer (of union, spiritual betrothal, and spiritual marriage) are a rare occurrence in this life? What do they require? How are they related? Does God call many to these stages of prayer or only a few? Would you like to have such experiences? Is it right to ask God for them?

Chapter Four

SAINT ALPHONSUS AND THE MANNER OF MAKING MENTAL PRAYER

L ike many Catholic spiritual writers before him, Alphonsus thought of mental prayer as a familiar conversation and between the soul and God.[1] This conversation was meant to be intimate and ongoing. It was also something that was relatively easy to understand and to integrate into one's life on a daily basis. Alphonsus was not the first Catholic author to write about the manner of making mental prayer (and certainly not the last). From the very outset, however, his approach was recognized for its simplicity, the ease with which it could be put into practice, and the emphasis it placed on the prayer of petition. In this chapter, we will examine the various components of Alphonsus's teaching on mental prayer and make some appropriate observations about its relevance for today.

THE APPROACH OF ALPHONSUS

Alphonsus lived at a time when there already existed a great variety of methods of mental prayer to choose from (for example, those of Ignatius of Loyola, Teresa of Ávila, Francis de Sales, John Baptist de La Salle, and the priests of Saint Sulpice).[2] These methods employed a variety of techniques for helping a person to foster in his or her life an intimate conversation with God. They were similar in that each contained (1) an element of reflection on a divine truth, (2) the application of the insights gained from this reflection to one's life, and (3) making a decision to do something about it.[3] Alphonsus used these same basic ingredients in his own approach to mental prayer. What set him apart was his creative and eclectic use of these other methods in order to custom-build an approach to mental prayer that was especially suited to his particular pastoral concerns.

Alphonsus treated the topic of mental prayer at least five times in his literary corpus, an indication of the important place it held in his overall pastoral strategy.[4] Even though he believed that everyone received sufficient grace to pray, he was utterly convinced that people needed instruction in the basics of how to carry on a close, intimate conversation with God. Mental prayer, in his mind, was the simplest and most expedient way of doing so. Without it, a person would be unable to pray as he or she ought. With it, that person was sure to enjoy a vital relationship with Christ. It was for this reason that Alphonsus considered mental prayer morally necessary for salvation. He developed his approach in order to reach as many people as possible. When compared to some of the other methods available at the time, it was simple, straightforward, and relatively easy to learn.

Alphonsus, we should note, preferred to speak of "the manner" rather than "the method" of making mental prayer.[5] He understood that the relationship between the human and the divine fostered in mental prayer could suffer from too much structure. To approach God with a ready-made, step-by-step recipe for intimacy could be a sign of disrespect and perhaps even a subtle form of manipulation. His method was really nothing more than a series of flexible guidelines that he had found from his own experience to be valuable tools in nurturing one's relationship with God. Taken together, the various elements of his manner of making mental prayer involved a person's body, emotions, intellect, will, spirit, and, when done in common as he strongly suggested, even community. During mental prayer, these important dimensions of human existence were opened up to God and laid bare. By expressing oneself in this way, a person manifested his or her dependence on God in a very concrete way. Recognizing one's need for God was the necessary first step in developing a vital, intimate relationship with the divine.

Alphonsus firmly believed that God wanted everyone to be saved and that teaching people the manner of making mental prayer was the best means at his disposal for ensuring that they were headed in the right direction. In developing his approach, he was especially indebted to Teresa of Ávila for the close connection she saw between prayer and love and to Francis de Sales for a simple schema that would eventually become even simpler. Alphonsus, one might say, followed the spirit of Teresa and simplified the schema of Francis de Sales to meet his particular pastoral concerns.[6] The result was an approach to mental prayer that could be taught to anyone, especially the poor, unlearned peasants whom he encountered on the back roads and in the forgotten villages of the southern Italian hill country.

THE MANNER OF MAKING MENTAL PRAYER

Alphonsus's manner of making mental prayer involves three distinct albeit intimately related movements: the preparation, the body of mental prayer itself, and the conclusion. A close look at each of these components will give us a better appreciation of the whole of Alphonsus's approach.[7]

1. *The Preparation.* During this time, we ready our bodies and minds to enter into mental prayer. To do so, we must put aside all extraneous thoughts and be careful not to allow our minds to wander. We should be kneeling (the preferable position) or sitting (if kneeling proves burdensome). The preparation itself consists of three distinct acts: (a) an Act of Faith in the presence of God, (b) an Act of Humility and Contrition, and (c) an Act of Petition for Light. Alphonsus gives us examples of how we can perform these prayerful actions. For the Act of Faith, we can simply pray: "My God, I believe that you are here present, and I adore you with all my soul."[8] We should be careful to pray this without distractions and with a lively faith. For the Act of Humility and Contrition, we can pray: "Lord, I should now be in hell in punishment of the offences I have given you. I am sorry for them from the bottom of my heart; have mercy on me."[9] For the Act of Petition for Light, we can pray: "Eternal Father, for the sake of Jesus and Mary, give me light in this meditation, that I may draw fruit from it."[10] Today, such acts could be simplified even more in the following way: "Lord, I believe in your presence" (Act of Faith). "I am sorry for my sins" (Act of Humility and Contrition). "Give me Light" (Petition for Light). Once we have turned to God in this way, we end our period of preparation by recommending ourselves to the Blessed Mother with a Hail Mary, to Joseph, to our guardian angel, and to our patron saint. These acts should be short but full of fervor so that we may immediately move on to the body of mental prayer itself.

2. *The Body of Mental Prayer.* The main body of mental prayer contains: (a) the meditation, (b) the affections, (c) petitions, and (d) resolutions.

a. The Meditation. When we meditate in private, Alphonsus encourages us to begin by reading a book and to stop whenever we find ourselves touched by a certain thought. At this point, we should raise our hearts to God so that we can receive the full benefits of the inspirations we have received. Only then should we return to the printed page and proceed to the next point. When we meditate in common, however, he states that one person should read for the whole group. When this occurs, the subject of the meditation is to be divided into two parts. The first part is read at the beginning, after the preparatory acts; the second, toward the middle of the half-hour or after the consecration if the meditation is done during Mass. The person reading should do so slowly and with a loud voice so that he or she can be easily understood. Alphonsus reminds us that the advantage of mental prayer comes not in the meditating, but in making affections, petitions, and resolutions. These, he says, are the principal fruits of meditation. He gives us a dictum of Saint Teresa, "The progress of a soul does not consist in thinking much of God, but in loving him ardently; and this love is acquired by resolving to do a great deal for him."[11] He goes on to describe meditation as the needle that must be threaded with the golden string of affections, petitions, and resolutions.

b. The Affections. After we have reflected on the point of meditation, Alphonsus instructs us to raise our hearts to God and to express whatever feelings or pious sentiments come over us. He encourages us to make acts of humility, confidence, or thanksgiving. Above all, we should make fervent acts of contrition and love. Such affections help bind the soul to God and enable us to overcome our faults. For Alphonsus, an *Act of Love* would go something like this, "My God, I esteem you more than all things. I love you with my whole heart. I delight in your happiness. I wish to see you loved by all. I desire only what you desire. Make known to me what you want from me and I will do it. Dispose of me and all that I possess as you see fit."[12] Today, we could simply say, "Lord, I love you with all my heart." To conform ourselves to God's will in this way involves a dying to self that is, at one and the same time, both an act of great virtue and act of martyrdom. Alphonsus encourages us to make every effort during holy prayer to unite our hearts to the will of God. He also reminds us of the difference between ordinary mental prayer and infused contemplation. The former involves our actions performed under the influence of God's grace, while the latter involves the direct action of God on the soul. His advice to us on this point is clear. Should we at any time feel united to God in this supernatural way, then we should not perform any acts other than those to which we feel ourselves drawn to God. Until we receive such a call, however, we should follow the ordinary method of mental prayer.

c. Petitions. During mental prayer, it is also very profitable for us to make frequent petitions to God for his graces. Such requests are to be made with humility and confidence. They are more useful to us than anything else we do at prayer. In particular, we should ask for the graces of light, resignation, perseverance, and especially the gift of love. By receiving God's love in our hearts, we have access to all other graces. We should repeatedly ask God for this precious grace, even at times of aridity and darkness. During such moments, all we have to say is: "My Jesus, mercy. Lord, for the sake of your mercy, assist me."[13] Today, we could simply pray: "Lord, help me." Even if that is all we can do, our prayer can be most useful and fruitful. Asking God for his graces is an essential part of mental prayer. In fact, such prayer consists of nothing else than acts of love and petitions for grace. He reminds us that mental prayer is the respiration of the soul. When we breathe, air is first taken in and then given back. In a similar way, the soul receives grace from God through its petitions and then gives itself to him through acts of oblation and love.

d. Resolutions. As the main body of mental prayer draws

to a close, it is important to make a particular resolution. This practical application of the Gospel to our lives may involve the decision to avoid a particular defect that we are prone to or to practice a virtue we are in need of. It may also involve suffering some annoyance or performing some act of penance. Whatever we decide upon, it should be something necessary for our ongoing conversion. We should repeat our resolution over and over until we have overcome the defect in question or acquired the virtue we were looking for. We should also commit ourselves to carrying out whatever resolutions we have made as soon as possible. At this time, we would do well to renew any vows or particular engagements that we have made to God or promised to do for him. Such a renewal will please God, help us to persevere in our commitments, and offer us new opportunities to grow in merit and grace.

3. *Conclusion*. The session of mental prayers ends with (a) thanking God for the lights we have received, (b) making a firm commitment to fulfill the resolutions we have made, and (c) asking God for the grace to remain faithful to Jesus and Mary. We should also recommend to God our brothers and sisters, both living and dead. As the day progresses, we should try to carry in our hearts one or two points that touched us in a special way. We should also try to live in the presence of God by making heartfelt prayers of love, resignation, and self-offering. We should not allow even fifteen minutes to pass without raising our hearts to God by some good act. Regardless of our situation, we should do our best to unite ourselves to God. We do so by observing silence, by seeking solitude as much as possible, by remembering the presence of God in our lives, and by preserving the sentiments of love that arose within us during our session of mental prayer.

Alphonsus's manner of making mental prayer could be used by just about anyone. It had the essential elements of the other methods of mental prayer (for example, consideration, application, and resolution), but was noted for its simplified, easy-to-learn structure, and the centrality that it gave to the prayer of petition. Although he sometimes used the terms mental prayer and meditation interchangeably, Alphonsus was well aware of the difference between the two. Meditation involved merely thinking about God, while mental prayer had to do with an actual conversation between the soul and God. Alphonsus was deeply conscious that the fruits of mental prayer came from the various affections, petitions, and resolutions that a person made after the beginning period of meditation.

ALPHONSUS'S EXTENDED TEACHING

Alphonsus offers us more than just a simple and practical way of conducting mental prayer. He also provides us with the theological reasons for understanding its importance. This theological context is just as important as the method itself—perhaps more. What follows is a brief summary of his extended teaching on this matter.[14]

1. *Mental Prayer Is Morally Necessary for Salvation.* In the first place, mental prayer enlightens the mind. It gives us a deeper knowledge of ourselves. It enables us to see our defects and imperfections. It also helps us to identify the remedies that will bring healing to our souls. When we meditate on the divine truths we are able to understand the importance of salvation and see more clearly what we must do to receive it. Second, mental prayer disposes us to practice the virtues. It makes our hearts tender and docile so that we can listen to the promptings of the Holy Spirit and respond to them in appropriate ways. It also gives us the strength to overcome temptation and to develop those habits of mind and heart that will draw us closer to God. Finally, mental prayer helps us to pray as we ought. God does not help us if we do not ask for his assistance. The importance of the prayer of petition highlights the moral necessity of mental prayer all the more. If we do not converse

with God in the depths of our hearts, then our relationship with him will weaken over time, and we will forget to ask for the graces needed to draw closer to him.

2. *Mental Prayer Is Indispensable in Order to Attain Perfection.* The saints became holy on account of their persistence and dedication in the practice of mental prayer. Alphonsus cites many saints as examples: Saint Vincent de Paul, Saint Catherine of Bologna, Saint Peter of Alcantara, Saint Philip Neri, Saint Aloysius Gonzaga, Saint Laurence Justinian, Saint John Chrysostom, Saint John Climacus, and many others. Saint Ignatius Loyola is attributed with the saying that mental prayer is the shortest way to attain perfection. Mental prayer is meant for everyone—not just priests and religious. It irrigates the soul. It fills a person with holy thoughts, affections, desires, and resolutions. Most importantly, it gives a person an intense love for God. The person who advances most in mental prayer makes the greatest progress in perfection. Those who persevere in its practice can make great strides in their own spiritual journey and, through the power of intercession, help others to do the same.

3. *The Ends of Mental Prayer.* In order to truly profit from the practice of mental prayer, it is important to understand its specific goals. The first end of mental prayer is to unite ourselves to God. To do so, it is not enough merely to think about God. We also need to make fervent acts of humility, confidence, self-sacrifice, resignation, contrition, and love. The perfection of love comes from conforming one's will totally to God. Those who complain that they pray but do not find God are not detached enough from the things of this world. To find God we must seek him in the solitude of our hearts. The second end of mental prayer is to obtain grace from God. We must meditate in order to avoid sin and to obtain those helps necessary for our salvation. When we pray, we should ask God especially for the grace of perseverance and the gift of his holy love. The third end of mental prayer is to discern God's will

for us. Alphonsus reminds us that we should not focus on the spiritual consolations that sometimes accompany the practice of mental prayer. Such delights are momentary and quickly fade. It is much more important for us to open our hearts to God and to seek his will, especially during moments of dryness and spiritual desolation.

4. *The Principal Subjects of Meditation.* Topics of meditation suitable for a session of mental prayer include the four last things: death, judgment, hell, and paradise. These truths cannot be seen with our physical eyes, but are perceived only by the soul. If we do not meditate upon them, we easily lose sight of them and act in ways that are detrimental to our welfare. Another important topic of meditation is our obligation to love God. We have received so many gifts from God. If we do not meditate upon them, however, we will ignore their presence in our lives and eventually forget about them. When that happens, we can easily draw false conclusions about our place in the world and overlook our duty to love God with all our heart, mind, soul, and strength. Generally speaking, we should meditate on those truths and mysteries that both touch and nourish us. By far, the subject most suitable for someone in pursuit of holiness is the Passion of our Lord. Doing so opens our eyes to the malice of sin and of God's mercy and love. Any aspect of the mystery of the Christ event can arouse in us deep sentiments of gratitude and love for God.

5. *The Place and Time Suitable for Meditation.* Alphonsus tells us that we can converse with God meditatively just about anywhere: at home, at work, when we travel, even while walking. The essential condition for mental prayer is not solitude of place, but solitude of heart, which amounts to maintaining a certain degree of detachment from worldly thoughts and affections. We can take this inner attitude of the heart with us wherever we go. For this reason, we can engage in mental prayer even when we find ourselves in the busiest of situations. Those whose vocation and livelihood bring them in close

contact with the bustling activities of the world can take heart from this message. Be that as it may, Alphonsus advises us to retreat to a solitary place when we engage in mental prayer. The best place for doing so is the church, for there we have the added advantage of having Jesus before us in the Blessed Sacrament. As far as time is concerned, Alphonsus focuses on two things in particular—the time of the day most suitable for making mental prayer, and the length of time we should devote to it. Although we can pray at all times and in all places, morning and evening are the two parts of the day most suited for mental prayer. The morning hours in particular are especially fitting. As far as the time to be spent in mental prayer, Alphonsus cites various examples from the lives the saints and then advises us to devote at least two hours a day to the practice of mental prayer. A half an hour a day, he claims, would be sufficient only for beginners.

6. *Distractions and Aridities.* Alphonsus tells us not to be disturbed by distractions. When they occur, we should not try to get rid of them by force, but remove them with gentle calm so that we can compose ourselves and quietly return to God. It is impossible to be free of all distractions. We should not be discouraged when they come, but should be intent all the more to turn our minds and thoughts to God. However great our distractions may be, we should never give up the practice of mental prayer. Involuntary distractions do not affect the benefits that come from mental prayer. When they are voluntary, we should catch ourselves, return our attention to God, and continue our prayer. In a similar way, we must resolve not to discontinue the practice of mental prayer during periods of aridity. The loss of a feeling of devotion and any sensible desire of loving God comprises some of the greatest pain any of us will face during meditation. As we mature in the spiritual life, the spiritual consolations that came to us earlier in our journey sometimes weaken and may even completely disappear. If this occurs, we should not take this as a sign of God's

displeasure with us, but as an opportunity for growth. True devotion consists not in feeling, but in our decision to promptly accept the will of God. In times of intense difficulty, we should divide our prayer time into several parts and ask God for help. In such periods, it is sufficient to say: "My Jesus, mercy. Lord have mercy on us."[15] During mental prayer we should seek only the light to know and the strength to accomplish God's will for us. Nothing else matters.

OBSERVATIONS

Alphonsus does more than merely instruct us in the manner of making mental prayer. He also tells us why it is important, what it does for us, where and when we should practice it, and how we should deal with specific difficulties. His teaching brings depth to the specifics and helps us to understand why mental prayer is so essential in fostering our relationship with God. Above all, he emphasizes the importance of its daily practice. Mental prayer is to the health of the soul as breathing is to the health of the body. Knowing about the benefits of mental prayer will gain us nothing if we fail to make it an integral part of our daily lives. The following remarks will focus on what we might do today to help this happen.

1. To begin with, we should consider changing its name from mental prayer to something like meditative prayer or discursive meditation. Alphonsus inherited the phrase, mental prayer, from the Catholic spiritual tradition. He used it to distinguish this quiet prayer form involving the active use of mind and heart from vocal prayer (which involved some kind of verbal expression) and contemplation (which in its infused form had God as its primary agent). Although he sometimes used them interchangeably, he also wishes to distinguish mental prayer from meditation, a term which, strictly speaking, involved only thinking about or reflecting on God. Today, the term mental prayer is no longer in vogue and seems to be a

hindrance to many people. Prayer involves the whole person and does not take place only in the mind.

2. Alphonsus's approach to mental prayer was noted for its simplicity. We forget sometimes that this characteristic applies to the very structure of the prayer itself. Over the years Alphonsus's method has been presented as a rigid format that must be closely followed and applied it all its details rather than as a series of flexible guidelines that will help people to converse with God more intimately. For Alphonsus, however, mental prayer was nothing more than the conversation that went on between the soul and God. He knew that if care was not taken, the structure he was presenting as an aid to prayer could get in the way of that conversation and perhaps even become an obstacle to one's intimacy with God. If Alphonsus's approach to mental prayer is to have relevance for us today we must hold it gently, take advantage of its flexible structure, and adapt to changing circumstances.

3. We must also remember that there is a strong contemplative dimension to Alphonsus's approach to mental prayer. Perhaps we were afraid of talking this way in the past because of Alphonsus's own concern for drawing a clear distinction between mental prayer (an activity of the person under the influence of ordinary grace) and infused contemplation (an activity of God in the person that takes place through the influence of extraordinary mystical grace).[16] Be that as it may, the close connection between meditation and contemplation in today's spiritual vocabulary should allow us to draw out this important dimension of Alphonsus's approach. Solitude of heart, for Alphonsus, was an essential condition for mental prayer. Without it, it would be impossible to converse with God with confidence and familiarity.

4. We should also note that Alphonsus's approach to mental prayer involves the whole person. All the various dimensions of human existence are taken into account. Alphonsus's consideration of proper posture and the most appropriate times

and places to practice mental prayer demonstrate his concern for the physical. His emphasis on reading and meditation as the point of departure for mental prayer shows his interest in the intellectual. The importance that he gives to the affections and to the will reveals sensitivity to the emotional and volitional. His insistence that solitude of heart form the experiential backdrop against which mental prayer takes place indicates a concern for the spiritual. Finally, his promotion of communal exercises of mental prayer and the importance he places on intercessory prayer addresses the social. Alphonsus's approach touches the physical, emotional, intellectual, volitional, spiritual, and social dimensions of human existence. When following his manner of making mental prayer, the whole person is actively engaged.

5. We should also remember to view Alphonsus's approach to mental prayer in the context of the various grades of prayer developed in the last chapter.[17] Alphonsus was keenly aware of these other forms of prayer and had a deep, personal experience of them—even the mystical grades. He focused on mental prayer, however, because he firmly believed that all people were called to it and that it was the most efficacious in helping them to foster an intimate relationship with God. For all the emphasis that he gave to mental prayer, however, Alphonsus also knew that God sometimes blessed people with even deeper experiences of intimacy (as in the mystical grades of prayer). He taught that one should cease making mental prayer at such times and allow the Lord to work in one's life directly through this intuitive face-to-face encounter.

6. In the light of the various grades of prayer, we should note that Alphonsus's manner of making mental prayer is actually a combination of meditation and affective prayer.[18] These two grades of prayer are actually two sides of the same coin: the former focuses on the intellect and the latter on the heart. Putting them together in this way enables him to emphasize the importance of integrating one's mind and heart. It also

leads him to emphasize the capacity to love as the essential element for determining a person's growth in holiness. Alphonsus made it very clear that mental prayer disposes the heart to the practice of the virtues. As the queen of the virtues, charity unites us with God and gives us a deeper, connatural knowledge of him. Because the end of Alphonsus's approach to mental prayer is to unite us to God, it follows that both mind *and* heart would play a significant role in the way it is carried out.

7. Alphonsus's approach to mental prayer is also noted for the central role it gives to the prayer of petition. To do so, we first have to delve deep within our hearts and make a concentrated effort to identify our needs. Only then can we express those needs to God and ask him for help. Alphonsus encourages us to express all of our needs to God, regardless of how trivial they may seem. We should take special care, however, to present our spiritual needs to God, especially our desire for the grace to lead holy and virtuous lives. Obtaining grace from God is an important end of mental prayer. Asking for it demonstrates our radical dependency on God and enables us to approach him with simple, childlike trust. Those who pray in this way cannot help but be drawn closer to God. God cannot befriend us, however, if we do not ask him to. The practice of mental prayer is a way of making sure that this process of asking becomes an integral part of our daily lives.

8. Finally, Alphonsus's approach to mental prayer provides us with the opportunity to develop in our lives an authentic Christian spirituality of practice. For him, mental prayer should be done on a daily basis. Through the repeated movements of preparation, meditation, affection, petition, resolution, and conclusion, the values of the Christian life become instilled and deeply rooted in us. Living this discipline of prayer helps us to become fervent disciples of Jesus Christ. Mental prayer produces concrete results in our lives: it leads us along the

way of conversion; it deepens our relationship with God; it helps us to see him in all things. The role of the resolution made during mental prayer has particular relevance in developing this spirituality of practice. Only by deciding to do something to make our yearning for God a concrete reality in our lives can we honestly say that we are cooperating with the movement of the Spirit in our lives.

These observations indicate just some of ways in which Alphonsus's manner of making mental prayer can be adapted to our present circumstances. Those seeking intimacy with God will find it both relevant to their needs and extremely rewarding.

CONCLUSION

Alphonsus's manner of making mental prayer was simple, flexible, and highly practical, something that could be taught to both simple and learned alike. He did not develop his approach in a vacuum, but relied heavily on those spiritual masters whose teachings on prayer had helped him the most in his own spiritual journey. What he came up with was a way of fostering an intimate relationship with God that could be practiced anywhere, by anyone, at anytime.

At the heart of Alphonsus's approach lies the need to retreat to the solitude of one's heart so that one can get in touch with one's deepest yearnings and express them to God. Asking God for help is a central feature of this manner of making mental prayer. When making these petitions, we are not telling God something that he does not already know, but simply getting in touch with our dependence on him for all things. Our recognition of this dependency puts us in touch with our ongoing need for conversion. Integral to this process is our need to make concrete resolutions of a practical order that will improve our relationship with ourselves, others, and God.

Alphonsus's approach to mental prayer has great relevance

for today. In it, he offers an easy and uncomplicated way of probing our hearts and expressing what we find there to God. Although certain adaptations to his approach would have to be made in order to respond to our present sensitivities, the substance of his teaching remains a valuable point of departure for anyone interested in nurturing their relationship with the Divine. Alphonsus believed that God's offer of plentiful redemption extended to everyone. His manner of making mental prayer provides us with a way of tapping into God's bountiful love for us so that even today that same love can become an integral and vital part of our daily lives.

REFLECTION QUESTIONS

1. For Alphonsus, mental prayer needs to take place against a backdrop of internal solitude. Why is such solitude so important for this kind of prayer? How does one attain it? Once found, what can one do to preserve it? Do you have an easy or difficult time settling down to prayer? Have you discovered any particular helps that you could share with others?

2. Do Alphonsus's suggestions for preparation for mental prayer make sense to you? Is there anything you would add or drop? How long a time should a person spend on this kind of preparation? How little is too little? How much is too much? Do you normally prepare yourself for prayer? If so, how do you go about it? If not, why not?

3. For Alphonsus, the body of mental prayer consists of a planned sequence of meditation, affections, petitions, and resolutions. In your experience, is this a good order to follow? Does it make sense? Is it simple enough to remember? What would happen if the order got mixed up? Would it affect the quality of your prayer? Does your conversation with other people always follow the same logical sequence? Should your conversation with God do so? What

are the dangers of turning Alphonsus's manner of making mental prayer into a strict method?

4. For Alphonsus, the conclusion of mental prayer should include an act of thanksgiving, a commitment to carry out one's resolutions, and a request for perseverance. Why are these necessary? Why do they come at the end of the period of prayer? Is there anything you would add or drop? How do you typically end your period of meditative prayer?

5. For Alphonsus, mental prayer was an essential tool for helping a person to foster an intimate relationship with God. Do you agree with him? Is it the only way of fostering this relationship or merely the simplest and most practical? Do you agree with all of his extended teaching on mental prayer? Is there anything in it that you would change?

Chapter Five

AN ALPHONSIAN MODEL
OF SPIRITUAL DIRECTION

Although Saint Alphonsus was a noted spiritual director, much of his teaching does not seem directly relevant to our present circumstances. In his day, spiritual direction was still closely tied to the sacramental ministry of the confessor. Today, it tends to be considered a ministry in its own right, one easily offered by priests, religious, and laity alike. Alphonsus's approach, moreover, was considerably directive and does not go well with the nondirective style that has become prevalent today.

The strength of a spiritual tradition, however, lies in its ability to adapt itself to changing circumstances. In this chapter, we will suggest that Alphonsian spirituality has a particular model of spiritual direction to offer that is both relevant and highly applicable to today's needs. That model, however, comes not from what Alphonsus taught about spiritual direction itself (although even there we still have much to learn from him),[1] but from a creative rereading of what he says about the manner of making mental prayer.

THE "HOW" OF MENTAL PRAYER

To summarize the main points of the previous chapter, mental prayer, for Alphonsus, "...is nothing more than a converse between the soul and God; the soul pours forth to him its affections, its desires, its fears, its requests, and God speaks to the heart, causing it to know its goodness, and the love which he bears it, and what it must do to please him."[2] He considers it essential for growth in the spiritual life. It enlightens our minds; it disposes us to practice the virtues; and it helps us to pray as we should. For these reasons, it is an indispensable part of our walk to holiness and can be considered morally necessary for salvation.

Mental prayer, according to Alphonsus, is not just for the select few. Anyone can do it, and everyone is called to it. It is also relatively easy to learn. It has a clearly defined beginning, middle, and end, what Alphonsus calls the preparation, the meditation itself, and the conclusion. In the *preparation*, the person praying affirms his or her faith in God's presence, makes an act of humble contrition, and requests enlightenment during the upcoming exercise. The *meditation* involves four movements: (1) reflecting on some aspect of the life of faith, (2) raising one's heart and affections to God, (3) asking God for help, and (4) making some practical resolutions to improve one's walk with the Lord. The *conclusion* consists of thanking God for the enlightenment received, affirming one's decision to carry out the resolution, and asking God for the grace of fidelity. At the end of each session, Alphonsus also encourages the one meditating to pray for others, especially the deceased and those hardened by sin.[3]

When properly carried out, this manner of making mental prayer can help a person to foster an intimate relationship with the Divine. It makes possible a dynamic encounter with God that involves an ongoing process of self-discovery, revelation of heart, request, and resolution. Interestingly enough, all of these elements are directly applicable to the ministry of spiritual direction in the Church today.

THE "HOW" OF SPIRITUAL DIRECTION

Alphonsus's guidelines for mental prayer can be taken as a metaphor for the spiritual direction process itself. Before we draw out the various parallels involved, let us add that projecting Alphonsus's method of mental prayer onto the plane of spiritual direction may contribute to the rediscovery of this important prayer-form among Redemptorists and the people they serve. One of the unfortunate by-products of the post-Vatican II era has been the general neglect by Redemptorists of the practice of individual and communal meditation. Incorporating Alphonsus's guidelines for mental prayer into the dynamics of spiritual direction will help them to draw important links between this particular facet of their spiritual heritage and their practice of this specialized ministry in the life of the Church. It will also offer hope to those who, for lack of guidance or misunderstandings about its purpose and scope, have had difficulties practicing Alphonsus's approach with regularity and conviction. When receiving spiritual direction according to the model that we are about to propose, a person's appreciation of Alphonsus's approach to mental prayer should deepen considerably.

1. *The Preparation.* Spiritual direction should always be preceded by a period of preparation. In addition to whatever the director and directee do privately, we suggest that they open a session of direction by sitting together in silence for a few minutes. As they do so, they bow their heads, assume a comfortable posture of prayer, and simply rest in the divine presence. When they have become sufficiently recollected, they should make brief acts of faith in God's presence, humility and contrition of heart, and a request for guidance. These acts can be done either quietly or out loud. If the latter, they should

occur at the end of the period of silence, just before the time for sharing begins. We can adapt Alphonsus's words to the direction process in this manner: "Lord, we believe that you are present with us during this period of direction" (Act of Faith in God's Presence). "Lord, we are sorry for our sins from the bottom of our hearts; have mercy on us" (Act of Humility and Contrition). "Dear Lord, give us light during this period of direction, that we may draw fruit from it" (Request for Guidance). However they are expressed, making these prayers at the start of the direction session helps both the director and the directee to recognize the sacredness of what is about to take place. It helps them to place God at the center of the process and to see that, without his help, they can do nothing. By acknowledging the presence of the Lord in this way, they prepare to engage in a dialogue that is not a mere exchange of ideas, but an encounter of holy listening where one discerning heart speaks to another. When the appropriate moment comes, they end the silence by praying together the doxology to the Lord's Prayer: "For Thine is the kingdom, the power, and the glory forever and ever. Amen."

2. *Spiritual Direction.* After the period of preparatory silence, the director and directee enter into the actual direction process itself. Following Alphonsus's guidelines for mental prayer, this process would include four distinct periods: meditation (what we will call "reflection"), affections, petitions, and resolutions. We will now demonstrate what each of these would look like in the context of spiritual direction.

a. The Reflection. Moving from silence into the direction period itself, the director invites the directee to engage in a process of reflection over the events since their last meeting. If the directee does not know where to begin, the director should reassure him or her that one place is as good as any other. When describing the manner of making mental prayer, Alphonsus encourages the meditative use of a book to get one going and to keep one from being distracted. One is to stop reading, however, when one finds oneself touched or inwardly moved. In spiritual direction, the directee should be encouraged to go over the book of his or her life. Recounting these events helps a person to gain perspective on them and possibly to receive deeper insights into their meaning. When the directee is moved by a particular event, he or she should be encouraged to look into the experience more deeply. The director should help the directee to reflect on the significance of the event through attentive listening, by finding connections with other things that have been shared, and by inviting the directee to look for God in the midst of these circumstances. During this time, the directee is more or less "unpacking" his or her life before the director and should be given the freedom to do so as he or she sees fit. The director, in turn, needs to listen carefully to what is being said, taking in not just the words themselves, but the intricate combination of bodily gestures, feelings, ideas, and silences, that contribute to making the directee's statements a unique revelation of self.

b. The Affections. After an appropriate period of reflection, the directee should be helped to focus on his or her feelings about what has been shared. Up until now, a significant effort has been made to unravel these events and to reflect upon their significance; it is now time to process them on the emotional level. In his guidelines for making mental prayer, Alphonsus encourages the person meditating to raise his or her heart to God with pious sentiments and acts of love. To do so authentically, however, a person must first be in touch with his or her feelings and recognize them for what they are. Many people cannot bring their emotions to prayer, because they are terribly out of touch with them. At this stage of the direction process, the director needs to help the directee to identify and express the various nuances of his or her experience. This would include one's reactions toward particular situations, as well as one's emotional stance toward oneself, others, and God. During this time, the director should help the directee to probe his or her feelings—both positive and negative—about the various issues that have been raised thus far during the direction session. This can be done through sensitive, nonthreatening questions that invite the directee to delve into and to try to understand the emotional side of his or her life. If the directee finds this difficult, the director might be able to help by suggesting a variety of possible emotional responses and then asking the directee to identify which comes closest to his or her experience. When the directee's feelings have been sufficiently examined, the director can say something like, "You have expressed these feelings and emotions to me, but have you ever expressed them to God?" *(Wait for a response.)* "Do you think you can?" *(Wait for a response.)* "Are you willing to try?" *(Wait for a response.)* In most cases, the directee will say that he or she will try to bring these feelings to God in prayer. Once this happens, the directee should be able to express the genuine affections of love to God indicated by Alphonsus.

c. The Petitions. As the process of spiritual direction continues, we are called to get in touch not only with our feelings but also with our needs. In his guidelines for mental prayer, Alphonsus emphasizes the importance of bringing our needs to the Lord and asking for his help. It is difficult to bring our needs to God, however, if we do not know what they are. At this point of the direction process, we are called to delve beneath our thoughts and feelings and to concentrate on what we need. When doing so, most of us will first focus on externals (for example, passing an exam, a problem at work, a raise in salary, and so on). While these are to be affirmed, the director should also encourage the directee to identify his or her interior needs as well (for example, patience, gentleness, compassion, and so on). On the deepest level, the directee should, in time, surface his or her need for God. The goal here is to be as honest with oneself and with one's director as possible. All of one's needs should be identified and taken possession of, regardless of how minor or insignificant they may seem. The director can help the directee in the identification process by mentioning the various anthropological dimensions of human existence—the physical, the emotional, the intellectual, the spiritual, and the social—and by reminding him or her that it is quite normal for us to have needs of various kinds. Once ample time has been given to discovering and taking possession of one's needs, the director should help the directee to recognize the even deeper need of expressing them to God. Scripture will be particularly helpful in this regard, especially those passages dealing with the importance of relying on God at all times and bringing our needs to him (for example, Mt 7:7–11; Mt 11:28–30; Jn 15:1–8).

d. The Resolutions. Once the directee has been helped both to probe his or her thoughts, emotions, and needs and to express them to God in prayer, the direction begins to wind down. In his guidelines for mental prayer, Alphonsus stresses the importance of making some practical resolutions that, through repeated effort, will help a person grow in virtue and holiness. In a similar way, the director should encourage the directee to look back over the discussion that has taken place during the past hour and identify some concrete practices that will help him or her to draw closer to God. The goal here is for the directee to take an honest look at his or her capabilities and to make a realistic decision about what next steps should be taken. The resolutions, in any case, must not be something imposed from without, but discovered and embraced from within. The process of spiritual direction focuses on the directee's unique relationship with God. As such, it should eventually lead him or her to an awareness of what concrete steps can be taken to strengthen that bond. The director's role here should be to help the directee to be as realistic as possible in forming appropriate resolutions. Care should be taken to avoid broad, sweeping generalizations such as "spending more time with the Lord" or "deepening one's prayer life." If the directee seems too vague or abstract in forming these resolutions, questions should be asked like, "Practically speaking, what does this mean for you?" or "How will this change your life?" Care must also be taken that the directee does not make a concrete resolution that is so demanding that he or she will have little hope of ever putting it into practice. It is much more desirable to make resolutions that lead to small incremental ways of deepening one's relationship with God than to formulate grandiose schemes that will never be seriously implemented. The goal here should be to help the directee ask honest questions about what he or she is capable of doing in trying to foster a deeper, more intimate relationship with the Divine. In this way, the director will foster in the directee a deep sense of the importance of the continuity between belief and action. This spirituality of practice will gently lead the directee along the way of conversion and, in time, enable him or her to orient every dimension of his or her life to the Lord.

3. *The Conclusion.* After the resolutions are made, the direction session should draw to a close, preferably through another period of silence. During this time, the director and directee gather into themselves all that has happened during their time together and thank the Lord for being with them. In the silence of the Word, they recognize the limitations of their feeble attempts to articulate their experience and appreciate the importance of listening to life's experiences with attentive care. In his guidelines for mental prayer, Alphonsus suggests that the meditation period conclude with three acts of prayer: (1) thanksgiving for the enlightenment received, (2) asking for help to fulfill one's resolutions, and (3) petitioning Jesus and Mary for the grace of faithfulness. In a similar way, the director and directee should use the silence at the end of the direction process to thank the Lord for the guidance received, to seek help in implementing the practical steps decided upon, and to ask for perseverance in the walk of discipleship. These prayers can also be verbalized at the end of the period of silence with the simple words, "Thank you, Lord, for guiding

us during this hour. Enable us to put what we have learned into practice. Help us always to remain faithful." Spoken or unspoken, such prayers allow the director and directee to affirm the Lord's involvement in their search for discernment. As they sit together in silence, they gain a stronger sense of the Lord's deep, attentive listening to their concerns. So deep is this listening that it contains within itself the unspoken beginnings of an articulated response. God's Word speaks to them in silence and sustains them in their struggle to make sense out of their lives. It follows them wherever they go and penetrates their experience from one moment to the next. When it is time to leave, they lift up their grateful hearts and repeat the same words with which they began the direction session: "For thine is the kingdom, the power, and the glory, forever and ever. Amen!"

OBSERVATIONS

Making Alphonsus's approach to mental prayer as the basis for a model of spiritual direction makes a great deal of sense. The following observations will demonstrate why.

1. For one thing, both involve conversation. Mental prayer, as described by Alphonsus, is the soul's intimate conversation with God. Spiritual direction, in turn, involves a dialogue between a director and his or her directee that focuses specifically on the directee's relationship with God. Since the purpose of spiritual direction is to deepen a person's intimacy with the Divine, it follows that the director will want to know how the directee relates to God, that is, how he or she prays. The great benefit of a model of spiritual direction based on the dynamics of the Alphonsian approach to mental prayer is that the various elements of a person's intimate conversation with God are transposed onto the direction process itself. The director, in other words, will be able to determine something about the quality of a person's relationship with God by the manner in

which the directee participates in the direction process. Directees, for example, who cannot be still, or who have a difficult time reflecting on their lives, identifying their feelings, expressing their needs, or making resolutions are likely to have the same difficulties in the way they relate to God. When seen from this perspective, the direction process gives the directee an opportunity to examine his or her conversation with God through the eyes of a skilled third party who is interested in it and who may be able to help him or her make it more intimate.

2. Like Alphonsus's approach to mental prayer, this model of spiritual direction is also simple and easy to learn. Directors and directees can grasp its key concepts with relative ease and implement them during the direction session with a minimum amount of trouble. The past twenty-five years has seen a great expansion in the number and quality of training programs in spiritual direction. Despite this great influx, however, many people still lament their difficulty in finding a good director. Perhaps this is so because spiritual direction is not only a science (which can be learned) but also an art (which is mostly a gift). Those who have the potential to be good spiritual directors will find in this model of direction a basic meat-and-potatoes approach to the ministry that will enable them to tap into their gifts and use them for the spiritual well-being of others. Directors trained in this model, moreover, will also be equipped with some important tools for understanding how they themselves relate to God. One of the strengths of this model is the way it introduces the dynamics of prayer into the direction process. Using this model teaches the director much about prayer, the direction process, and the relationship between the two.

3. Like Alphonsus's approach to mental prayer, this model of spiritual direction is active and discursive. The dialogical nature of mental prayer means that the person praying must play an active role in the way he or she relates to God. Even

though grace is required in both, mental prayer differs from the mystical states of prayer in that the person takes on an active rather than passive posture toward the mystery of the Divine. The various acts involved in this dynamic process (meditation, affections, petitions, resolutions) demonstrate the manner in which such activity occurs. In a similar way, the model of direction we are proposing also involves a high degree of activity. With the help of the director, the directee delves beneath the surface of his or her life and engages in an active search for meaning. From beginning to end, the process of direction demands active listening and honest sharing on the part of both participants. The conversation between them has a sacred, almost solemn, character to it. This active dialogue, moreover, should eventually move the directee toward some kind of decision about the next step that needs to be taken in his or her relationship with God.

4. Like Alphonsus's approach to mental prayer, this model of spiritual direction offers a flexible structure that can be adapted to specific circumstances. Alphonsus preferred to speak about "the manner" rather than "the method" of making mental prayer. He also recognized that too much structure could get in the way of a person's intimate and familiar conversation with God. Introducing the dynamics of mental prayer into the direction process allows this same flexibility to enter into the director/directee relationship. During a session of direction, the director must take special care not to allow the guidelines provided by this particular model to dictate the nature and tone of the conversation. Instead, the director must focus all of his or her attention on the directee and make sound prudential judgments about what questions to ask and which way the discussion should be steered. At all costs, he or she should avoid giving the impression that every session must follow a preordained format. The guidelines presented in this model are intended to facilitate the direction process, not get in its way.

5. Like Alphonsus's approach to mental prayer, this model of spiritual direction engages the whole person. Every dimension of human existence is in some way involved: the physical, the emotional, the intellectual, the volitional, the spiritual, and the social. During the direction session, the directee must feel free to raise any or all of these important aspects of life. The director should listen, moreover, for which topics the directee consistently fails to mention and to bring these omissions to his or her attention at the appropriate moment. If over a period of time the directee does not avert to one or more of these dimensions in his or her conversation with the director, there is a good possibility that he or she is failing to bring them to God in prayer. The director should help the directee to identify both the strengths *and* weaknesses in his or her anthropological makeup and create an atmosphere of trust that will allow him or her to explore those areas more freely. In doing so, the directee will come to a better degree of self-understanding and eventually be able to acknowledge them in his or her relationship with God.

6. Like Alphonsus's approach to mental prayer, this model of spiritual direction values the importance of fostering a contemplative attitude toward life. For Alphonsus, mental prayer must take place against the backdrop of what he calls solitude of heart.[4] Without this important disposition of the soul, it is impossible to hold an intimate conversation with God. Spiritual direction must take place against a similar backdrop of solitude. The physical surroundings in which the direction session takes place should be free of unnecessary noise and external distractions. More importantly, those involved in direction should foster an inner attitude of prayerful reflection that will enable them to find the presence of God in the simple events of the day. There are different degrees of inner solitude. The deeper a person journeys into this sacred internal sanctum, the more intimate will his or her conversation with God become. In a similar way, the more a person receiving direction

fosters a contemplative attitude toward life, the more will he or she benefit from the direction process.

7. Like Alphonsus's approach to mental prayer, this model of spiritual direction must be understood within the larger context of a person's ongoing spiritual journey. Important and necessary as it is for a person's relationship with God, mental prayer is but one of many grades of prayer (neither the highest nor the lowest).[5] Although it should be an important element of a person's way of relating to God, there may come a time when it must be put aside so that God can bless that person with an even deeper level of spiritual experience (for example, one of the mystical grades of prayer). Similarly, this model of spiritual direction does not claim to be the only approach to the ministry (or even the best, for that matter). Nor does it presume to be suitable for everyone or even for every stage of a person's life. When considering whether one should enter direction, it is very important to find a director with an approach that is most suitable for oneself. Directors, moreover, would do well to have experience in several approaches so that they could adapt themselves to the exigencies of the directees under their care.

8. In the light of the above, knowing when to continue the practice of mental prayer and when to let it go is extremely important, but rarely easy. The same is true for the spiritual direction process. The Holy Spirit is the spiritual director par excellence. As a person matures spiritually over time, the Lord may ask him or her to put direction aside, even if for just a while. The mature Christian should be able to respond directly to the promptings of the Spirit without having to interpret its signs through the intermediary of a director. If and when the directee is called to do so, it is usually because he or she has internalized the dynamics of the direction process to such a degree that he or she knows almost instinctively what to look for and what questions to ask in any given situation. At all costs, the director should be careful not to foster any unhealthy

relationships of dependence in his or her directees. Spiritual direction is a helping relationship, an aid to spiritual growth—not an end in itself. Directors should give their directees the freedom to discontinue the relationship and should even encourage them to do so if the relationship does not bring about authentic spiritual growth.

These are just some of the reasons why introducing the dynamics of mental prayer into the process of spiritual direction makes a great deal of sense. They are not the only reasons, but they are by far the most compelling and those most likely to have an impact on the ministry at large.

CONCLUSION

Using Saint Alphonsus's guidelines for the manner of making mental prayer the basis for a model of spiritual direction has many advantages. For one thing, it presents a viable approach to the ministry of spiritual direction in the Church today, one that is practical, easy to remember, and potentially beneficial to a great many people. It also offers a distinctive approach to this important ministry that is both highly creative also deeply rooted in the Alphonsian tradition. This correlation between the dynamics of mental prayer and spiritual direction also makes a great deal of sense.

It is appropriate that a Redemptorist approach to spiritual direction should have direct parallels with a prayer-form so zealously promulgated by Alphonsus. The whole purpose of spiritual direction, after all, is not unlike the goal of mental prayer itself: to help a person to draw closer to God. This approach to spiritual direction should strengthen rather than diminish interest in this particular approach to prayer. Each of these practices, moreover, reflects different (albeit related) spheres of the spiritual life: one focuses specifically on conversing with the Lord; the other, on examining one's relationship with the Lord in a prayerful manner. Because of their close structural resemblance, the practice of one should reinforce the practice of the other—and vice versa.

This model of spiritual direction will matter very little, however, if Redemptorists themselves do not take the time to ponder it, take ownership of it, and implement it in their ministry. To do so, they need to maintain an ongoing dialogue with the past so that helpful parallels can continue to be discovered between their rich spiritual tradition and the exigencies of their ministry. Redemptorists have much to be grateful for in the heritage bequeathed to them by Saint Alphonsus. In many areas of their life, the process of transforming their founder's insights into practical and relevant structures for today's ministry has only just begun. As this process continues, Redemptorists need to be creative, yet watchful. They must take to heart Jesus' admonition to his disciples to act "like the master of a household who brings out of his treasure what is new and what is old" (Mt 13:52).

REFLECTION QUESTIONS

1. Do you agree with the idea of using Alphonsus's approach to mental prayer as the basis for a new model of spiritual direction? If not, why not? What are the advantages and disadvantages of this new model? How does it differ from the approach used by Alphonsus during his own lifetime? If you were in the position to do so, would you offer direction in this way? Would you be willing to receive it?

2. Does it make sense to begin a session of direction with a period of silence and some brief acts of faith, contrition, and a request for guidance? Would doing so add anything to the process to follow? Would it take anything away from it? Why is such preparation important? What would happen if it were left out?

3. According to this model, direction consists mainly of a fourfold process of reflection, affection, petition, and

resolution. Is this process comprehensive enough? Flexible enough? Too highly structured? Does it address every dimension of a person's anthropological makeup? Is anything missing from it?

4. Does this model offer an adequate way of concluding a direction session? Can you think of a better way of ending a session? Is there anything you would add or drop? Does the parallelism between the preparatory and concluding moments add or detract from the direction process? Can the parallelism be improved in any way? Does it need to be?

5. What is the relationship between prayer and spiritual direction? Do you think this model of direction will impart to those who use it a deeper appreciation of the dynamics of mental prayer? If so, how will it do so? Will the process it promotes help a person pray any better? Could it hinder a person's life of prayer in any way? Can this model be used even when a directee is experiencing higher grades of prayer? If not, what alternative would you use?

Chapter Six

SOME PRACTICAL CONCERNS

Alphonsus's strong pastoral focus and his concern for the practical side of the spiritual life leads us in this closing chapter to look at the actual implementation of this new approach to spiritual direction. We will do so by going through the process again—step by step—and by making appropriate observations of a more pragmatic nature. The purpose of this chapter is to flesh out the process so that directors will have a sense of how to deal with situations that are likely to come up during the direction session. Moving from the abstract to the concrete in this way should ease some of the anxiety they might feel about using this approach in their ministry. It should also give them confidence in the viability of this model as a useful tool in helping others to become themselves in their faith.

THE DIRECTION PROCESS: SOME PRACTICAL CONCERNS

Going over the direction process with a sharp eye for possible snags and practical difficulties gives us the opportunity to deepen our own understanding of what spiritual direction is all about. At the very outset, it is important for us to remember that the primary focus of direction is to help a person come closer to God. This concern must be at the center of every stage of the direction process.

1. *The Preparation.* Both director and directee need to prepare themselves for the direction session that is about to take place. They should go through this preparation both together and alone. In the previous chapter, we have emphasized the importance of beginning the session with a period of silence during which time both director and directee can sit still in the presence of the Lord. This quiet reflection should help them to recognize the presence of the Lord in their midst (act of faith in God's presence), admit their need for God's mercy (act of humility and contrition), and ask for enlightenment throughout the entire process of direction (request for guidance). Just as important, however, if not more so, is the private time that each of them sets aside to get ready personally for the session. Practically speaking, each needs to find some time before their meeting to look back in a prayerful manner on what happened during the previous session. Each must also get in touch with the movement of the Spirit in his or her life during the intervening period of time. Finally, each must ready himself or herself for the session that is about to take place. All of this preparation should take place privately before they meet for the direction session itself. The director does so to be better able to place personal issues aside and thus to be of better help to the directee during the upcoming session. The directee uses this private period of preparation to allow issues to surface that he or she will bring to the direction session. To a large extent, the quality of the direction session will be a function of the serious personal preparation that both director and directee have brought to it. Although the time allotted for this private preparation will vary from person to person, it seems that a minimum of fifteen to twenty minutes for an examination of consciousness should be set aside at some point prior to each session. This remote preparation on the part of the director and

directee will make the proximate preparation at the outset of the session even more poignant and meaningful. It will also help them to focus more fully on the matters being discussed and thus make better use of the time at their disposal.

2. *Spiritual Direction.* These practical comments about the proximate and remote preparation for the direction session now lead us to make similar comments concerning the various aspects of the direction process itself. These elements include: (a) the reflection, (b) the affections, (c) the petitions, and (d) the resolutions.

a. The Reflection. As pointed out in the previous chapter, the purpose of the meditative aspect of the direction process is to help the directee go over the book of his or her life and to focus on certain key occurrences that have special meaning for understanding his or her relationship with God. During this part of the process, the director should exercise the discipline of active listening. Practically speaking, this discipline first involves emptying oneself as much as possible of all unnecessary distractions. It then means taking in the intellectual content being shared by the directee and absorbing the various emotions that goes along with it. Finally, it means reflecting these rational and affective dimensions back to the directee and helping him or her to find appropriate experiential parallels in the Scriptures and living tradition of the Church. Such active listening should have a liberating effect on the directee and enable him or her both to delve deeper into his or her experience and to sift through it with special attention to what God might be trying to say through it. All during this time, the director should remember that the reflective element of the direction session is only the first step in a much wider process. He or she must be careful not to allow the directee to get stuck on the intellectual level or to discount his or her feelings as merely secondary concerns that have little to do with one's relationship with God. What is more, the director needs to be aware of the appropriate time for leading the directee away from reflective emphasis on the book of his or her life to a more concentrated focus on bringing whatever feelings have surfaced during this first step of the direction process. Since there is no clear-cut way of knowing when to move the process of direction along, the director will often have to rely on his or her knowledge of the directee and an intuitive sense of where the Spirit might be leading them in the direction process. The director should also be aware that the real issue needing to probed and examined in the directee's relationship with God might be something very different from what is initially presented. The purpose of active listening at this stage of the direction process is to allow the directee's feelings to surface so that the deeper issues involved in his or her relationship with God may move from the periphery to the center of his or her awareness.

b. The Affections. As pointed out in the previous chapter, the purpose of the affective aspect of spiritual direction is to help the directee to process his or her feelings that have surfaced during the previous step. The goal here is to help the directee first to identify those feelings, then to name them, take ownership of them, understand them, and finally express them to God in prayer.[1] In addition to active listening, the director at this stage of the process may need at various times to suggest the wide range of feelings the directee may be experiencing. This holds true especially for those who are out of touch with their emotions or who have a difficult time articulating them. To accomplish this task, the director needs to show empathy toward the directee so that he or she will not feel judged or threatened in any way. Participating in another's feelings in this way is a sign of compassion. It helps the directee to feel safe to explore the various feelings that have surfaced thus far in the direction session and to deal with them in a constructive manner. The directee may need to be reminded at this point that, regardless of how we identify them, feelings are of themselves neither right nor wrong. It is how a person deals with them that will affect his or her relationship with the self, with others, and ultimately with God. Practically speaking, the director needs to do everything possible to create an atmosphere of trust that will help the directee to probe his or her feelings so that they can be openly aired during the direction session and eventually expressed to God. To do so, director and directee alike must be honest about the wide range of feelings (often mixed) that pass through their hearts. Only by being truthful with oneself about what one has been feeling, can a person take the further step of expressing them to God and thereby grow in intimacy with him. This stage of the direction process is geared toward helping the directee to increase his or her level of emotional self-disclosure.[2] At all times, the director should be gentle and extremely careful not to force the directee to share what he or she may not be ready for or totally willing to do.

c. The Petitions. As pointed out in the previous chapter, the purpose of the petitionary aspect of the direction process is to help a person to get in touch with his or her needs and then express them to God. Those needs should cover every aspect of a person's anthropological makeup: the physical, the emotional, the intellectual, the spiritual, and the social. At this stage of the process, the director may need to help the directee to distinguish authentic needs from merely apparent ones. To do so, it is important for the directee to have a sense of the direction he or she wishes to move in life on these various levels. While every authentic need should be identified and expressed, the director should encourage the directee to focus on those within easy, practical reach. Genuine human growth usually occurs in small increments. The director should help the directee to focus on those needs that will enable him or her to take the next significant step along the path to wholeness. Only by focusing on such needs will the directee eventually gain the confidence to reach out and ask for more. Helping the directee to focus on needs is an important way of surfacing his or her underlying need for God. When talking about needs during the direction session, the director should also emphasize that bringing our needs to God is a way of expressing our love for him. At appropriate times, he or she should also remind the directee that God needs our love and ardently desires to dwell within our hearts. "Paradise for God is...the human heart."[3] This phrase of Alphonsus expresses this need well and can be used by the director as a way of emphasizing God's deep desire to know everything about us. Scripture passages which emphasize the importance of bringing our needs to God (for example, Mt 7:7–11; Lk 11:2–4) and the Spirit helping us to pray (for example, Rom 8:26–27) can also be mentioned at appropriate times and used to great effect.

d. The Resolutions. As pointed out in the previous chapter, the purpose of making resolutions during the direction session is to help the directee to identify some concrete practices that will enable him or her to draw closer to God. Even though God alone is capable of ultimately transforming our lives, each of us has the responsibility of cooperating with his grace. Making a resolution to change a certain attitude of mind or way of acting demonstrates our willingness to work with the movement of the Spirit in our lives. The resolutions made during the direction session should be realistic and practical. They should also be in keeping with the directee's vocation within the Church (for example, priest, religious, lay) and should affirm rather than work against the various responsibilities associated with it. The director, moreover, should warn the directee not to bite off more than he or she can chew. It would be much better to make a small resolution that one has a good chance of keeping than to formulate an extensive plan that one will have little hope of ever implementing. The job of the director at this stage of the process is to enable the directee to come up with an appropriate set of resolutions that can be carried out and also be of genuine help to the directee in leading a holier and more virtuous life. These resolutions should be from the directee or at least wholeheartedly accepted by him or her. The director should take special care not to force the directee either directly or indirectly. If the directee has difficulty coming up with something, the decision to postpone making the resolution for a later time is also a possibility. If this is the case, the subject should be raised at a later time. A continuous pattern of postponements, however, should be brought to the directee's attention at the appropriate time and dealt with so that the underlying issues preventing him or her from deciding upon a proper course of action can rise to the surface.

3. *The Conclusion.* As pointed out in the previous chapter, the conclusion of the direction should consist of a period of silence during which time the director and the directee give thanks to God, ask for help in carrying out whatever resolutions have been made, and pray for the grace of perseverance. This time of silence allows the director and directee to acknowledge God's quiet presence throughout the entire session. Just how long this period should be is a matter of judgment. Much depends on what went on during the session itself and the level of sharing that took place. One or two minutes would seem to be a good rule of thumb, although, as a concluding prayer, the period of quiet could be lengthened or shortened at the discretion of the director. If it seems appropriate, the director can initiate some spontaneous vocal prayer that touches on something that took place during the direction session itself. He or she should be careful, however, not to fill the silence with too many words. During this time, the backdrop of silence that fills their lives must be allowed to come to the fore and shape them. The director and directee should allow their spirits to rise within them and to sip the silence that laps upon the interior shores of their souls. It is there, in the silence, where they listen—be it only for a while—to the still small voice of God within their hearts. When the director senses that the silence has washed their souls in the quiet presence of the Spirit, he or she brings the direction to an end in the usual manner.

As pointed out in the previous chapter, this model of spiritual direction suggests that every session begin and end with a period of silence. The practical value of beginning and ending in this way should not be overlooked. These bookends of quiet place a certain reflective distance between the direction session and the rest of life, thus giving both director and directee some perspective on what is about to take place and allowing them to make better use of the time they have set aside for their conversation. They also help the director and directee to acknowledge the presence of the Holy Spirit in their lives, the silent third partner of their conversation, without whose pervading influence the direction session would bear little (if any) spiritual fruit.

OTHER PRACTICAL MATTERS

In addition to those practical concerns immediately related to the direction process itself, a number of others pertain to questions about implementation, training, ongoing education, and the like. What follows is not an exhaustive list, but a sampling of some of the more obvious ones related to this particular model of direction.

1. As far as introducing a person to this particular model of direction is concerned, directors should be up-front with their directees from the start. In an initial meeting dealing with expectations, the director would do well to talk about his or her particular approach to the direction process. If the directee thinks that this particular approach is suitable to his or her needs, they should agree to begin a relationship of spiritual direction on a trial basis. A considerable amount of time should be given to this initial period (at least three months). During this time, the director listens to the directee and leads him or her through the process. The focus should at all times be on helping the directee draw closer to God. After the designated period of time, they should evaluate together both the model

and the director/directee relationship and decide how they should proceed.

2. It is also important to remember that the structure of this model of spiritual direction is meant to be flexible. One should not worry, therefore, if not every step in the process occurs in precisely the same order as it has been outlined above. A good director should learn the various steps of the model and try to incorporate them as much as possible into the direction session. At the same time, he or she should also be able to adapt the process to fit the circumstances of the moment. There will be times when it will not be possible to go through all the steps of the process during the time allotted for the session. When such moments occur, it is important for the director to discern the needs of the moment and to bring the process to an appropriate point of closure. To do so, he or she needs to have a prudent knowledge of his or her own capabilities, as well as a solid grasp of the needs of the person he or she is directing.

3. For the above reason, the director is strongly advised to be knowledgeable in a number of approaches to spiritual direction.[4] It would be presumptuous to think that a single model of direction would be able to cover every conceivable contingency. There will be times when an aspect from one model will be of use to the director as he or she tries to meet the needs of the directee. While the director should adopt one model as his or her overriding paradigm, he or she should be ready to incorporate elements from others as the need arises. This creative eclecticism is in keeping with the Alphonsian tradition and with the pastoral principle of doing whatever is necessary to draw others closer to God.[5]

4. Seminars, workshops, and training sessions should be set up to introduce experienced directors to this new model. These should be led by directors who themselves are familiar with the Alphonsian tradition and able to explain the transposition of relationships that takes place between Alphonsus's manner of making mental prayer and the model itself. In addition to

the theoretical dimension of the model, special emphasis should be given to the various benefits it can afford them and the practical ways in which they can introduce it into their ministry. In time, certificate programs could be set up that would ensure that the quality of the instruction given and the training received.

5. Even though the director should use the model flexibly and be willing to complement it from time to time with elements of other approaches, he or she still needs to monitor the process so that it is not unnecessarily going off track. Very often, the director will need the help of an outside observer to ensure that he or she is being faithful to the direction process. Being a part of an ongoing process of individual or group supervision can be of tremendous help in enabling the director to reflect back upon a particular session and to see if anything got in the way of the process. For this to happen, supervisors would need to be trained in this particular model of spiritual direction and able to point out the various strengths and weaknesses of a particular director's implementation of it.

6. However, if the director chooses to associate the sacrament of reconciliation with a direction session in any way, then it would be advisable to maintain strict confidentiality at all times. To protect the seal of confession, the director would do well not to share anything that went on during the entire direction session with anyone, not even a supervisor. Even though names are normally changed in a supervision session to protect directees, even the slightest possibility that a third party might be able to surmise the identity of the person confessing his or her sins should be enough to convince the priest-director to maintain strict confidentiality. Priests should be aware of the need to maintain strict confidentiality whenever they associate spiritual direction with sacramental reconciliation.

7. At the same time, there are many benefits to be reaped by associating spiritual direction with sacramental reconciliation. As pointed out in previous chapters, the connection

between the two, while not intrinsic, goes deep within the tradition of the Church.[6] If, in the past, direction normally occurred after one had confessed their sins so that a priest could help the directee make greater strides in holiness, perhaps today it could be used to help people come back to the sacrament of reconciliation. Today, many people may need to talk about their life of faith (or lack of it) before they will be ready to open their hearts to God and seek forgiveness for their sins. When done properly, spiritual direction may be a way of helping people to maintain their connection with this important sacrament.

8. In any case, priest-directors should be advised to maintain a flexible stance toward the relationship between spiritual direction and sacramental reconciliation. Usually, the best thing to do is to leave it in the hands of the directee. When expectations are dealt with at the outset of a direction relationship, the directee should be advised of the opportunity of having the sacrament and that the desire to receive it should be made known to the priest-director at the beginning of a session. Some directees may never take advantage of it. Some may do so often, either at the beginning or at the end of the session. Some may wait a long time before asking. The directees should be helped to understand the difference between direction and sacramental reconciliation, but also shown that there are occasions when the two can and should go together.

9. Those directors who are not priests and who therefore cannot conduct the sacrament of reconciliation during a direction session should carry out their ministry in a spirit of collaborative referral. If the occasion arises when a directee expresses the need to go to confession, the director should direct him or her afterwards to a priest in the locality who will promote the direction process rather than hinder it. This form of collaboration between nonordained spiritual directors and priest-confessors needs to be developed much more, especially if the practice of spiritual direction is to serve as an

instrument of bringing people to take more advantage of the healing graces associated with the sacrament. Priests, in turn, need to be more fully aware of the great service done to the life of the Church by nonordained spiritual directors and be willing to work with them in this important work of collaborative referral.

10. Steps should be taken, moreover, to ensure that directors receive sufficient continuing education in this model. These measures should take place on two levels. First, discussions should take place that will help the model to develop to its fullest potential. It is one thing to propose a model of direction based on the transposition of relationships in a particular model of mental prayer. It is quite another thing to round out the rough edges and to improve the dynamics and inner workings of the process itself. In addition to the theoretical level, efforts should be made to help directors to improve those skills that are most needed in the successful implementation of this model. Seminars in active listening, for example, using role models and the analysis of particular case studies could be of great help to directors interested in maintaining in their ministry a high quality of professional competence.

11. In line with the above, efforts could be made to explore the possible adaptation of this model to group direction. The basis for this suggestion comes from the great value that Alphonsus placed on meditation in common.[7] If community meditation was so highly esteemed by the early Redemptorist communities, perhaps the same process of preparation, reflection, affections, petitions, resolutions, and conclusion could be extended to a small group of six or seven people under the supervised care of an experienced director. Perhaps the session itself could begin with a twenty-minute period of common meditation. What happened within each person during that time could then become the starting point for the direction session itself.

12. Finally, some concerns should be raised about fees and

how they relate to this particular model of direction. It is becoming more and more common in the ministry of spiritual direction for directors to ask some form of payment from their directees (usually one hour of a person's daily wage). Priest-directors who allow sacramental reconciliation during a direction session should avoid giving any impression that they are asking for money in return for the sacrament. To avoid any possibility of impropriety, they would do well to avoid asking for any kind of monetary remuneration for their services. Nonordained directors are freer to suggest some type of payment. They should remember, however, that the Alphonsian tradition has a strong pastoral focus on reaching out to the poor and most abandoned. All laborers in the Lord's vineyard deserve to be compensated for their labors. Care must be taken, however, to preserve the central focus of the tradition upon which this particular model of spiritual direction is based. Perhaps the time has come for Redemptorist parishes and retreat centers to hire qualified lay spiritual directors as part of their salaried staff.

This brief list of practical concerns is intended as a help to directors who might be interested in implementing this model of spiritual direction in their ministry. Although it is by no means an exhaustive catalog of the difficulties that might arise, it does offer some general suggestions about how each step of the direction process should be carried out and how one should deal with a number of possible trouble spots. It should also be added that they are meant to serve only as suggestions and are thus subject to revision as more and more directors reflect upon their experience of the model as a useful tool for helping others to draw closer to God.

CONCLUSION

Concluding this book with a treatment of practical considerations is entirely in keeping with the spirit of Alphonsus. In his own day, no one was more concerned than he with developing and implementing pastoral strategies that responded to the concrete spiritual needs of those living on the margins of society. That same concern should motivate those seeking to follow in his footsteps. This exercise of historical correlation seeks to do so by adapting Alphonsus's pragmatic concern for quality pastoral care to the ministry of spiritual direction in the post-Vatican II era. The transposition of Alphonsus's approach to mental prayer to this field offers an innovative model of spiritual accompaniment that is in keeping with the Alphonsian tradition and able to respond to many of the deep spiritual hungers voiced in the world today.

This approach to direction gives a person the opportunity to examine every level of his or her relationship with God. Taking place against a contemplative backdrop of silence, it focuses on the thoughts, feelings, needs, and practical steps needed for a person wishing to draw closer to God. Because it is based on the inner dynamics of Alphonsus's approach to mental prayer, it can also help a person to arrive at a better understanding of what it means to converse with God intimately—and with open heart. This close connection between spiritual direction and the dynamics of prayer should come as no surprise. Teaching people how to pray always had an important place in Alphonsus's pastoral strategy. To look to his manner of making mental prayer for some insight into the process of spiritual direction underscores the close correlation between the two.

The process of spiritual direction involves the transposition of the way a person relates to God onto the director/directee relationship. Doing so enables a person to better understand the various strengths and weaknesses in the manner in which he or she addresses God. Using Alphonsus's simple and straightforward approach to mental prayer as the basis for a new model of spiritual accompaniment not only makes a great deal of sense but also holds much promise for the ongoing development of this venerable Christian ministry. Firmly rooted in both the teaching and the spirit of Saint Alphonsus, it has great potential and practical significance for the bearers of his spiritual legacy and the people they are called to serve.

REFLECTION QUESTIONS

1. Do you agree that director and directee need both remote and proximate preparation when using this model of direction? Does the suggested time of fifteen to twenty minutes for remote preparation for a session seem too much or too little? What is important here: the time itself or how that time is spent?

2. In addition to active listening, what other practical skills does a director need when trying to implement this model? Are any of these skills unique to this model of direction? Is it a skill to be able to move with a person from the level of reflection, to the expression of one's feelings, to identifying one's needs, and deciding upon some course of action?

3. What practical function does the concluding moment of silent and/or spontaneous prayer serve in the direction process? Does one or two minutes seem adequate? During that time how does one balance the need for silence with one's desire to give thanks to God, to ask him for help, and to express one's desire for perseverance?

4. What difficulties would you expect to face when implementing this model of direction for the first time? Can you anticipate any snags? How serious are they? Do you think they can be avoided? If not, how would you deal with them? What advice would you give to someone who is thinking about adopting this particular approach to direction?

5. Can you think of any other practical matters concerning the implementation and ongoing use of this model of direction?

Are there any other practical observations regarding supervision, ongoing training, or the adaptation of this model to group direction? Are you satisfied with the observations made concerning the relationship of this model to sacramental reconciliation? How would you handle the delicate question of payment?

PRAYER TO THE HOLY SPIRIT (II)

Holy Spirit, Divine Paraclete, Father of the poor, consoler of the afflicted, light of hearts, sanctifier of souls! Behold me prostrate in your presence. I adore you with the most profound submission, and I repeat a thousand times with the seraphs who are before your throne: Holy, Holy, Holy! I firmly believe that you are eternal, consubstantial with the Father and the Son. I hope that by your goodness you will sanctify and save my soul. I love you, O God of love! I love you more than all the things of this world. I love you with all my affections, because you are infinite goodness that alone merits all love. And since, insensible as I have been to you holy inspirations, I have been so ungrateful as to offend you by so many sins, I ask you a thousand pardons for them, and I supremely regret having ever displeased you, O sovereign good! I offer you my heart cold as it is, and I ask you to let a ray of your light and a spark of your fire enter within to melt the hardened ice of my iniquities. You who have filled with immense graces the soul of Mary, and inflamed with a holy zeal the hearts of the apostles, promise also to set on fire my heart with your love. You are a divine Spirit; fortify me against evil spirits. You are a fire; enkindle in me the fire of your love. You are a light; enlighten me so that I may know eternal things. You are a breath that is full of sweetness; dissipate the storms that my passions raise up against me. You are a tongue; teach me the manner of praising you without ceasing. You are a cloud; cover me with the shadow of your protection. And if, finally, you are the author of all heavenly gifts, ah, I ask you to grant them to me. Vivify me by your grace. Sanctify me by your charity. Govern me by your wisdom. Adopt me by your bounty as your child. Save me by your infinite mercy. May I never cease to bless you, to praise you, to love you during my life on earth and for all eternity. Amen.

ALPHONSUS DE LIGUORI

NOTES

INTRODUCTION

1. This threefold distinction comes from Richard E. Palmer, *Hermeneutics* (Evanston, Ill.: Northwestern University Press, 1961), 13.
2. For example, still to be completed is the multi-volume series *Opere Ascetiche*, eds. O. Gregorio, G. Cacciatore, and D. Capone (Rome: Sant'Alfonso, 1933–).
3. See, for example, Théodule Rey-Mermet, *Alphonsus Liguori: Tireless Worker for the Most Abandoned*, trans. J.-M. Marchesi (Brooklyn, N.Y.: New City Press, 1989); Frederick M. Jones, *Alphonsus de Liguori: The Saint of Bourbon Naples, 1696–1787* (Liguori, Mo.: Liguori Publications, 1999).
4. See Alphonsus de Liguori, *The Complete Works of Saint Alphonsus de Liguori*, ed. Eugene Grimm, 22 vols. (New York: Benzinger, 1886–97; reprint ed. Brooklyn, St.Louis, Toronto: Redemptorist Fathers, 1926–27). [NB: This work is based on the 27-volume French translation of the Italian published by Leopold Dujardin and Jules Jacques]; Carl Hoegerl, ed., *Heart Calls to Heart: An Alphonsian Anthology* (Rome: Sant'Alfonso, 1981, *ad usum privatum*); Frederick M. Jones, ed., *Alphonsus de Liguori: Selected Writings*, in The Classics of Western Spirituality (New York/Mahwah, N.J.: Paulist Press, 1999); Alphonsus de Liguori, *The Practice of the Love of Jesus Christ*, trans. Peter Heinegg (Liguori, Mo.: Liguori Publications, 1996); idem, *The Glories of Mary* (Liguori, Mo.: Liguori Publications, 2000).

CHAPTER ONE

1. For a variety of definitions of spiritual direction, see Dennis J. Billy, "The Relations of Spiritual Direction," *Studia moralia* 36 (1998): 67 n. 1.
2. Steve R. Wigall, "History's Role in Defining Spiritual Direction,"

Review for Religious 57 (1998): 67. For a helpful (but by no means complete) presentation of the history of spiritual direction, see Kenneth Leech, *Soul Friend: The Practice of Christian Spirituality* (San Francisco: Harper & Row, 1977), 34–89.

3. The quotation comes from Wigall, "History's Role in Defining Spiritual Direction," 68. See also Tilden Edwards, *Spiritual Friend* (New York: Paulist Press, 1980): 92. For types of spirituality, see Philip Sheldrake, *Spirituality and History*, new edition (Maryknoll, N.Y.: Orbis Books, 1995, 196-221.

4. For the rise and influence of auricular confession, see John Mahoney, *The Making of Moral Theology: A Study of the Roman Catholic Tradition* (Oxford, England: Clarendon Press, 1987), 1–36. For the difference between spiritual direction and confession, see Jordan Aumann, *Spiritual Theology* (London: Sheed and Ward, 1980; seventh impression, 1993), 381–82. See also Leech, *Soul Friend*, 194–225.

5. For the *hesychast* tradition in Eastern Orthodoxy, see *The Study of Spirituality*, Chesyln Jones, Geoffrey Wainwright, and Edward Yarnold, eds. (London: SPCK, 1992), 235–76.

6. For the origins of the pastoral counseling movement, see Leech, *Soul Friend*, 90–136. For the relationship between pastoral counseling and spiritual direction, see *The New Catholic Dictionary of Spirituality*, ed. Michael Downey (Collegeville, Minn.: The Liturgical Press, 1993), s. v. "Pastoral Care and Counseling" by Raymond Studzinski.

7. For a presentation of spiritual direction in the contemporary climate, see *The New Catholic Dictionary of Spirituality*, s. v. "Spiritual Direction" by Carolyn Gratton.

8. Wigall, "History's Role in Defining Spiritual Direction," 68.

9. Many of these traditions are developed in Lavinia Byrne, ed., *Traditions of Spiritual Guidance* (Collegeville, Minn.: The Liturgical Press, 1990). See also Kevin G. Culligan, ed., *Spiritual Direction: Contemporary Readings* (Locust Valley, N.Y.: Living Flame Press, 1983), 167–229.

10. Bernard of Clairvaux, *Apology to William of Saint Thierry*, IV.8 (PL 182.903–4). Cited in John Paul II, *Vita consecrata*, no. 52.

11. A look at a recent directory of Spiritual Directors International shows a strong ecumenical dimension and large lay component in its membership. See *SDI Membership Directory, July 1998* (San Francisco, CA: Spiritual Directors International, 1998).

12. John Paul II, *Novo millennio ineunte*, no. 43.

13. The term *transposition* simply means "the putting of the higher into the lower." See John R. Sheets," Spiritual Direction in the Church," *Review for Religious* 46 (1987): 506. For the transposition of Trinitarian relationships onto the director/directee relationship, see Gerald E. Keefe, "Letter to a Person Beginning Spiritual Direction," *Review for Religious* 33 (1974): 542.

14. *The New International Webster's Comprehensive Dictionary of the English Language*, 1996 ed., s. v. "tradition."
15. Ibid., s. v. "commune," "communion."
16. For the levels of spirituality, see Walter H. Principe, "Toward Defining Spirituality," *Studies in Religion/Sciences religieuses* 12 (1983): 135–37; *The New Catholic Dictionary of Spirituality*, s.v. "Spirituality, Christian," by Walter H. Principe.
17. This definition is adapted from Ronald Rolheiser, *The Holy Longing: The Search for a Christian Spirituality* (New York: Doubleday, 1999), 5–12.
18. For varying degrees of incorporation in the Church, see *Lumen gentium*, nos. 13–17. For spiritual direction in Protestant traditions, see Leech, *Soul Friend*, 78–88. For spiritual direction in non-Christian religions, see Byrne, ed., *Traditions of Spiritual Guidance*, 165–210.

CHAPTER TWO

1. For references to this debate, see Principe, "Toward Defining Spirituality," 129, esp. n. 3.
2. For the various levels of spirituality (that is, experiential, doctrinal, analytical), see chap.1 n.16. For an application of these levels to Alphonsus, see Dennis J. Billy, *Plentiful Redemption: An Introduction to Alphonsian Spirituality* (Liguori, Mo.: Liguori Publications, 2001), 98–101.
3. Alphonsus de Liguori, *Prayer, The Great Means of Obtaining Salvation and All the Graces Which We Desire of God* in *The Complete Works of Alphonsus de Liguori*, ed. Eugene Grimm, vol. 3, *The Great Means of Salvation and Perfection* (New York: Redemptorist Fathers, 1886–94; reprint ed., Brooklyn, St. Louis, Toronto: Redemptorist Fathers, 1927), 49.
4. Ibid., 19–22.
5. Alphonsus de Liguori, *Mental Prayer and the Exercises of a Retreat* in *The Complete Works of Alphonsus de Liguori*, ed. Eugene Grimm, vol. 3, *The Great Means of Salvation and Perfection* (New York: Redemptorist Fathers, 1886–94; reprint ed., Brooklyn, St. Louis, Toronto: Redemptorist Fathers, 1927), 252–58.
6. Alphonsus de Liguori, *The Way to Converse Always and Familiarly with God* in *The Complete Works of Alphonsus de Liguori*, ed. Eugene Grimm, vol. 2, *The Way of Salvation and Perfection* (New York: Redemptorist Fathers, 1886–94; reprint ed., Brooklyn, St. Louis, Toronto: Redemptorist Fathers, 1927), 395.
7. Alphonsus de Liguori, *The Practice of the Love of Jesus Christ* in *The Complete Works of Alphonsus de Liguori*, ed. Eugene Grimm, vol. 6, *The Way Holy Eucharist* (New York: Redemptorist Fathers,

1886–94; reprint ed., Brooklyn, St. Louis, Toronto: Redemptorist Fathers, 1934), 456.

8. Alphonsus de Liguori, *Prayer, The Great Means of Obtaining Salvation*, 240.

9. See, for example, Pope Pius XI, "Allocuzione del 20 Settembre 1934," in *Annuarium Apostolatus Orationis* (Rome, 1935), 73. See also *Dizionario di Mistica* (Rome: Libreria Editrice Vaticana, 1998), s. v. "Alfonso Maria de Liguori (santo)" by G. Velocci.

10. For the patriarchal and matriarchal influences on Alphonsus's temperament and character, see Marciano Vidal, "La famiglia nella vita e nel pensiero di Alfonso de Liguori (1696–1787)," *Studia moralia* 32 (1994): 355–62.

11. For a presentation of Alphonsus's early life, see Frederick M. Jones, *Alphonsus de Liguori: The Saint of Bourbon Naples, 1696–1787* (Dublin: Gill & Macmillan, 1992), 7–23. For an influence of Alphonsus's family on his life and thought, see Vidal, "La famiglia nella vita e nel pensiero di Alfonso de Liguori (1696-1787)," 341–66.

12. After his first communion, Alphonsus became a member of the Sodality of Young Noblemen under the patronage of Saint Joseph. When he finished his university studies in 1715, he graduated to the Sodality of Our Lady of the Visitation (for university graduates). Both sodalities were under the direction of the Oratorians, see Jones, *Alphonsus de Liguori*, 14–15, 24–25.

13. For a list of his personal favorites, see Joseph W. Oppitz, *Alphonsian History and Spirituality: A Study of the Spirit of the Founder, Saint Alphonsus M. Liguori and of the Missionary Institute, The Congregation of the Most Holy Redeemer* (Rome/Suffield, Conn.: Privately published [ad usum privatum], 2d printing, 1978), 28.

14. This summary of the schools of Christian spirituality that influenced Alphonsus comes from Oppitz, *Alphonsian History and Spirituality*, 29–32.

15. The phrase "creatively eclectic" comes from Oppitz, *Alphonsian History and Spirituality*, 28.

16. On Mary's mediating role in our salvation, see Alphonsus de Liguori, *The Glories of Mary*, in *The Complete Works Saint Alphonsus de Liguori*, ed. Eugene Grimm, vols. 7–8 (New York: Redemptorist Fathers, 1886–94; reprint ed., Brooklyn, St. Louis, Toronto: Redemptorist Fathers, 1931), 152–78.

17. For the theological and pastoral dimensions of Alphonsus's Marian devotion, see Hamish F. G. Swanston, *Celebrating Eternity Now: A Study of the Theology of Saint Alphonsus de Liguori* (Chawton Alton Hampshire: Redemptorist Publications, 1995), 220–30.

18. For spiritual direction in Alphonsus's correspondence, see Sean Wales, "The Ministry of Spiritual Direction: Saint Alphonsus, the Spiritual Director as Seen though His Letters," in *Reflections on the Spirit of*

Saint Alphonsus, ed. M. O'Shea (Monroe, Mich.: IHM Publications, 1987), 93–107.

19. Emilio Lage, "S. Alfonso e la direzione spirituale," *Spicilegium historicum CSSR* 48 (2000): 22–25.

20. Alphonsus de Liguori, *Praxis confessarii ad bene excipiendas confessiones*, chap. 1 in *Theologia moralis*, Vol. 4 (Rome: Typis Polyglottis Vaticanis, 1912; reprint 1953), 528.

21. Lage, "S. Alfonso e la direzione spirituale," 14 [my translation].

22. Oppitz, *Alphonsian History and Spirituality*, 30.

23. Bernard of Clairvaux, *Apology to William of Saint Thierry*, IV.8 (PL 182.903). Cited in John Paul II, *Vita consecrata*, no. 52.

24. See above n. 9.

CHAPTER THREE

1. For an analysis of the various dynamics involved in this approach, see Billy, "The Relations of Spiritual Direction," 67–94.

2. For a discussion of these categories, see Romano Guardini, *Prayer in Practice*, trans. Leopold of LoewensteinWertheim (New York: Pantheon, 1957), 120–57. For the last two categories, Guardini prefers the terms "inward" and "mystic" prayer.

3. The presentation of the nine grades of prayer is based on the summary of the Teresian teaching found in Jordan Aumann, *Spiritual Theology* (London: Sheed and Ward, 1980; seventh impression, 1993), 316–57. See also A. Poulain, *The Graces of Interior Prayer*, 10th ed., trans. Leonora L. Yorke Smith (London: Routledge & Keegan Paul, 1950), 7–58. In her own works, Teresa's teaching on the various grades of prayer is dispersed throughout *The Way of Perfection* and *The Interior Castle*. See *The Complete Works of Saint Teresa of Jesus*, ed. and trans. E. Allison Peers, vol. 2 (New York: Sheed & Ward, 1946). For Alphonsus's teaching, see *Pratica del confessore per ben esercitare il suo ministero*, nos. 99–122 (Modena: Tipografia Pontificia ed Arcivescovile "Immacolata Concezione," 1948), 160–89. For Alphonsus's fidelity to Teresa's ascetical and mystical doctrine, see Lage, "S. Alfonso e la direzione spirituale," 37.

4. Teresa of Ávila, *Life*, chap. 8 in *The Complete Works*, vol. 1, p. 50.

5. "Although Saint Teresa of Ávila does not use the expression *affective prayer* in any of her writings, she does refer to this grade of prayer, and it has been accepted by all schools of spirituality." See Aumann, *Spiritual Theology*, 324.

6. "The three stages or degrees of charity are nothing more than divisions that characterize in a general way the infinite variety of aspects in the Christian life. The path of the supernatural life is a winding path, and its stages offer a variety of transitions and levels

that will differ with each individual. We must never think that the three basic stages are self-contained compartments, and that those who are at a given time in one stage will never participate in the activities of another stage." See Aumann, *Spiritual Theology*, 115–16.

7. For a brief synthesis of Teresa's teaching, see Teresa of Ávila, *The Interior Castle*, The Classics of Western Spirituality, trans. Kieran Kavanaugh and Otilio Rodriguez, with an Introduction by Kieran Kavanaugh (New York, Ramsey, Toronto: Paulist Press, 1979), 21–29.

8. For Alphonsus, vocal prayer, mental prayer (in both its discursive and affective variety), and acquired contemplation ("ozio contemplativo") fall under the category of the ascetical life. The five grades of mystical prayer (nos. 5–9 above) he refers to respectively as "il raccoglimento," "la quiete," "l'unione semplice," "lo sposalizio," and "il matrimonio spirituale." See Alphonsus de Liguori, *Pratica del confessore*, nos. 99–122, pp. 160–189. For a treatment of Alphonsus's nuanced and somewhat restrained understanding of acquired contemplation, see Antoon Rosen, "La 'contemplation acquise' et la purification du sens dans la *Praxis confessarii* de S. Alphonse," *Spicilegium historicum CSSR* 48 (200): 49–108.

9. In meditation one seeks God with the effort of mental discourse, while in contemplation, one has already found God and contemplates him without effort. In meditation, moreover, the soul works through its own proper powers, while in contemplation God is the primary agent and the soul merely receives the gifts that are infused into it by grace. See Alphonsus de Liguori, *Pratica del confessore*, no. 104, p. 166.

10. For the contemplative dimension of Alphonsus's method of mental prayer, see Billy, *Plentiful Redemption*, 29–30.

11. Alphonsus de Liguori, *Prayer, The Great Means of Salvation*, 201.

12. Ibid., 49.

13. Alphonsus de Liguori, *The Way to Converse Always and Familiarly with God*, 391.

14. Alphonsus de Liguori, *Mental Prayer and the Exercises of a Retreat* in *The Complete Works*, 252.

15. For an expanded treatment of the characteristics of Alphonsian prayer, see Billy, *Plentiful Redemption*, 3–20.

16. See Alphonsus de Liguori, *Prayer, The Great Means of Salvation*, 19.

17. This is a slight modification of the definition of spiritual direction given in Jean LaPlace, *The Direction of Conscience* (New York: Herder and Herder, 1967), 26

18. See A. Muccino, "La dottrina mistica di S. Alfonso," *Rassegna di ascetica e mistica* 22 (1971); 214–38; Idem, "La vita mistica do S. Alfonso," *Rassegna di ascetica e mistica* 22 (1971): 309–16.

CHAPTER FOUR

1. Here are some examples from the Christian spiritual tradition of prayer as a loving dialogue with God: "Saint Gregory of Nyssa said that 'prayer is a conference or conversation of the soul with God.' Saint John Chrysostom said that 'prayer is discussion with divine majesty.' Saint Thomas Aquinas wrote: 'For friends to converse together is the proper condition of friendship. People's conversation with God is through contemplation.' Saint Francis de Sales wrote: 'Prayer is a colloquy, a discussion, or a conversation of the soul with God. By prayer we speak to God and God in turn speaks to us. We aspire to him and breathe in him; he reciprocally inspires us and breathes upon us.' Finally, there is Saint Teresa of Ávila's classic description: 'Prayer is nothing other than an intimate friendship. It is a frequent heart to heart conversation with him by whom we know ourselves to be loved.'" Cited in Pat Collins, *Intimacy and the Hungers of the Heart* (Dublin/Mystic, Conn.: Columba/Twenty-Third Publications, 1991; reprint ed. 1992), 190 [For the references to these quotations from the saints, see notes 2–6 on pp. 206–7]. For an appropriate parallel in the writings of Alphonsus de Liguori, see *The Way to Converse Always and Familiarly with God*, 391–417.
2. For a presentation of these methods of mental prayer, see Giacomo Lercaro, *Metodi di orazione mentale* 2d ed (Genoa/Milan: Bevilaqua & Solari/ Editrice Massimo, 1957), esp. 5, 91, 120, 146, 171, 216.
3. See Aumann, *Spiritual Theology*, 322.
4. These occur in *Homo apostolicus*, Appendix 1, nos. 2–5; *Praxis confessarii*, chap 9, nos. 122–25; *Pratica del confessore*, chap. 9, nos. 100–3; *La Vera sposa di Gesu Cristo*, chap. 15; and *Regolamento di vita di un Cristiano*, no. 2. The last provides only a very brief treatment. [Note: The original titles of these works have been retained in this instance for uniformity's sake. Three of the five do not appear in the English Grimm edition.] See also Lercaro, *Metodi di orazione mentale*, 121n.1.
5. See, for example, Alphonsus de Liguori, *The True Spouse of Jesus Christ*, in *The Complete Works*, ed. Eugene Grimm, vols. 10–11 (New York: Redemptorist Fathers, 1886–94; reprint ed., Brooklyn, St. Louis, Toronto: Redemptorist Fathers, 1929), 457.
6. See Lercaro, *Metodi di orazione mentale*, 111.
7. The following summary of Alphonsus's manner of making mental prayer comes from Alphonsus de Liguori, *Mental Prayer and the Exercises of a Retreat*, 273–84. See also, Alphonsus de Liguori, *The True Spouse*, 457–66.
8. Alphonsus de Liguori, *Mental Prayer and the Exercises of a Retreat*, 274; Alphonsus de Liguori, *The True Spouse*, 457.

9. Ibid.
10. Ibid.
11. Ibid., 276, 459.
12. Ibid., 277, 460.
13. Ibid., 279, 461.
14. The following summary of Alphonsus's extended teaching on mental prayer comes from Alphonsus de Liguori, *Mental Prayer and the Exercises of a Retreat*, 252–73, 281–84. See also, Alphonsus de Liguori, *The True Spouse*, 441–57.
15. Alphonsus de Liguori, *Mental Prayer and the Exercises of a Retreat*, 284; Alphonsus de Liguori, *The True Spouse*, 465.
16. For Alphonsus's distinction between mental prayer and infused contemplation, see his *Pratica del confessore*, no. 104, p. 166.
17. See chapter three under the subheading, "The Grades of Prayer," nos. 1–9.
18. Ibid., nos. 2–3.

CHAPTER FIVE

1. For Alphonsus's teaching on spiritual direction, see chapter two under the subheading, *On Leading Others to God*. See also Lage, "S. Alfonso e la direzione spirituale," 9–48.
2. Alphonsus de Liguori, *Mental Prayer and the Exercises of a Retreat*, 266.
3. See chapter four under the subheading, "The Manner of Making Mental Prayer."
4. Alphonsus de Liguori, *Mental Prayer and the Exercises of a Retreat*, 269.
5. See chapter three under the subheading, "The Grades of Prayer," nos. 1–9.

CHAPTER SIX

1. Five things are necessary for emotional self-awareness: "to notice, name, own, understand, and express our feelings." See Collins, *Intimacy*, 49. I have adapted this insight to the spiritual direction process by emphasizing the importance of expressing our feelings to God.
2. Along with "loving attention," "self-disclosure" is considered an essential element of interpersonal intimacy. See Collins, *Intimacy*, 126.
3. Alphonsus de Liguori, *The Way to Converse Always and Familiarly with God*, 395.
4. See, for example, David L. Fleming, "Models of Spiritual Direction," *Review for Religious* 34 (1975): 351–57; Sandra Schneiders,

"The Contemporary Ministry of Spiritual Direction," *Chicago Studies* 15 (1976): 127–29; Fabio Giardini, "The Many Roles of the Christian Spiritual Helper," *Angelicum* 65 (1988): 195–223.

5. The phrase "creative eclecticism" is adapted from Oppitz, *Alphonsian History and Spirituality*, 28 [cf. chap. 2 n.15].

6. For the historical relationship between spiritual direction and sacramental reconciliation, see Leech, *Soul Friend*, 194-225 [cf. chap. 1 n. 4].

7. For Alphonsus's teaching on meditation in common, see chapter four under the subheading, "The Manner of Making Mental Prayer." See also Alphonsus de Liguori, *Mental Prayer and the Exercises of a Retreat*, 276. Common meditation was a frequent practice in the early Redemptorist communities.

SUGGESTED READINGS

Billy, Dennis J. *Plentiful Redemption: An Introduction to Alphonsian Spirituality*. Liguori, Mo.: Liguori Publications, 2001.

Colón León, Jorge Raphael. *The Apostolate of Prayer: The Spiritual Message on the Prayer of Petition According to St. Alphonsus Maria de Liguori, the Apostle of Prayer*. San Juan, PR: The Redemptorists, 1989.

Fearon, N. and C. Farell, eds. *The Love of Jesus Christ*. Liguori, Mo.: Liguori Publications, 1987.

Hoegerl, Carl, ed. *Founding Texts of Redemptorists: Early Rules and Allied Documents*. Rome: Sant'Alfonso, 1986.

_____. *Heart Calls to Heart: An Alphonsian Anthology*. Rome: Sant'Alfonso, 1981 (a*d usum privatum*).

Jones, Frederick M. *Alphonsus de Liguori: The Saint of Bourbon Naples 1696–1787*. Liguori, Mo.: Liguori Publications, 1999.

_____ (ed.) *Alphonsus de Liguori: Selected Writings*. The Classics of Western Spirituality. New York/Mahwah, N.J.: Paulist Press, 1999.

Oppitz, Joseph. *Alphonsian History and Spirituality: A Study of the Spirit of the Founder, Saint Alphonsus M. Liguori and of the Missionary Institute of the Most Holy Redeemer*. Rome/Suffield, Conn.: Privately published (*ad usum privatum*), 2d printing, 1978.

_____. *Alphonsus Liguori—The Redeeming Love of Christ: A Collection of Spiritual Writings*. Brooklyn, N.Y.: New City Press, 1992.

Sutton, William A. "An Exposition of St. Alphonsus Liguori's Doctrine on Spiritual Direction." STD Dissertation. Rome: The Pontifical University of St. Thomas, 1978.

Rey-Mermet, Théodule. *Moral Choices: The Moral Theology of Saint Alphonsus Liguori*. Translated by Paul Laverdure. Liguori, Mo.: Liguori Publications, 1998.

_____. *St Alphonsus Liguori: Tireless Worker for the Most Abandoned*. Translated by Jehanne-Marie Marchesi. Brooklyn, N.Y.: New City Press, 1989.

Steingraber, John, ed. *Prayer Is Love*. Liguori, Mo.: Liguori Publications, 1973.

Swanston, Hamish F. G. *Celebrating Eternity Now: A Study in the Theology of Saint Alphonsus (1696–1787)*. Chawton Hampshire, Great Britain: Redemptorist Publications, 1995.

Wales, Sean. "The Ministry of Spiritual Direction: Saint Alphonsus, The Spiritual Director, as Seen through His Letters," pp. 91–107 in *Reflections on the Spirit of Saint Alphonsus Liguori*. Edited by Margaret M. O'Shea. Monroe, Mich.: IHM Publications, 1987.